Shelter in Place

The Write People

ISBN: 9798736675302

Marjorie Bleam, Diane Crane, Barbara Miller,
Peter Philander, Janet Feldman

The Write People

Born out of a larger group that disbanded at the pandemic, a small number of us fled to meet weekly on Zoom. Little did we know that the decision would keep us writing, keep us socializing and keep us sane while social distancing. During the months since the arrival of the pandemic, our little group has bonded and exchanged not only stories, but daily challenges and frustrations. We are all incredibly grateful for the support of each other, which has helped us deal with the months of isolation, and in some ways, fended off the loneliness that accompanies this epic virus.

Given the effects that Covid-19 has had on all of us, Peter, with an eye toward history and impact, thought it worthwhile to gather our pandemic stories and make them available to others. No doubt the reader will find within these pages relatable emotions and situations. It is our hope that they will provide some measure of comfort to all of us who have survived.

Table of Contents

The Middle of the Journey

By Peter Philander

At this moment in the pandemic, we should evaluate where we stand in the encounter with Covid-19. Soon a vaccine will be available, but the rate of infection rises relentlessly and rapidly.

The common factors for life on earth are DNA and RNA. DNA is mostly contained in the nucleus of cells and RNA in the cytoplasm with messenger
RNA going in between.

When we trace evolution back to the beginning of life on earth, it is clear that the first organisms consisted of one cell or they were viral. Cellular organisms have a nucleus containing DNA, while viral organisms have only RNA, and they tag along with cells and borrow their DNA to propagate themselves. As organisms evolved and grew more complex, unicellular and viral organisms continued to flourish. As life forms became more sophisticated and as multicellular organisms developed, viruses and unicellular organisms tagged along with them.

Each complex life form has a microbiome. This term describes the organisms that live in or on that animal or plant. Human beings have as many of these life forms as they have cells.

The process of evolution has been going on for many millions of years. For a comparatively short part of that time, perhaps the most recent ten thousand years or so, our species has been dominant. As we have multiplied in number and as we have moved, explored and exploited the earth, we have caused the eradication of many other species.

In addition to having RNA and DNA, all life shares the characteristic that it wants to continue and wants to create new life forms in its own image. Humans want to create babies; elephants want baby elephants and viruses want more viruses. When there is not enough grass for elephants, they move, or they die out. When the host of a virus disappears or goes extinct, the virus will find another host. Since mankind is widespread, we are at risk of being alternate hosts.

That is how coronavirus Covid-19 landed on us. And other viruses are, similarly, going to invade our species in the future because our activities eradicate other species which are their primary hosts. For a virus, a good host is one that lets both organisms thrive. If the host gets sick and dies, the virus must move and find another host. Through November 30th, 2020 the total number of infected people in the world is more than 63 million, and nearly one and a half million people have died.

Covid-19 infection is associated with a mortality rate of around 2%. In terms of the mortality it has caused, it rivals war. In Vietnam 60,000 American men died. In the second world war, half a million. To date, more than a quarter of a million fatalities have been reported in the United States. The virus is spreading and propagating on a vast scale and is doing so very rapidly. Winter in the northern hemisphere is a crucial time in our coping with this plague. While we are close to having vaccines for wide-spread use, infection rates, as well mortality rates, are increasing rapidly.

During the initial stages of the pandemic, our public health authorities recommended handwashing and maintaining sterile surfaces as the main method of control. At that time, it was said that masks were not effective. More recently it has been recognized that Covid is spread by suspension in the air. Infection from virus deposited on surfaces is less important.

We in the United States now enter the season when the weather forces us to spend most of the time indoors. Closed, sealed environments greatly increase the risk of the virus spreading from person to person. When somebody who carries the virus exhales, a cloud of invisible viruses is expelled into the air. When a person becomes infected, they are often without any symptoms for the first two days of the infection. Others never develop symptoms. Thus, there is a large group of people who feel completely healthy but are shedding the virus with each breath.

An unsuspecting new host inhales the air that the infected person breathes out and becomes infected. The only way to avoid this, if we must be indoors, the circulating air must be filtered and cleaned frequently. Fresh air and rapid changing of the air decreases the risk of inhaling suspended viral particles.

Wearing a mask greatly decreases the number of viruses that are exhaled. A secondary advantage is that the mask also decreases the number of particles that are inhaled.

The methods used to control spread of the virus have been widely publicized during the past year. We are tired of those rules. But this is also the moment when the need to obey the rules is greatest. Our hospitals are rapidly filling up with sick patients and our ICU's are similarly stretched.

Those who are most vulnerable need to shelter in place and to limit exposure. The eldest and most infirmed members of the population, who live in nursing homes and similar facilities, have been isolated and separated from the rest of society for nearly a year. Those institutions have had the most outbreaks of infection. By the law of unintended consequences, those individuals have also been experiencing the most severe social and emotional problems due to their being cut off from meaningful interaction with others. It is entirely appropriate that the new vaccines will first be used in those places and by those workers.

Less dramatic sheltering in place, causes less loneliness. For these people, it would be useful to start thinking about a chart of exposure. Each individual should maintain a scoresheet that shows the degree of risk taken each day. Staying at home and not talking to anybody face to face scores zero. Going out of the house will score a varying number based on the duration of time, the place visited e.g., the store, how many people are encountered, whether people are wearing masks and the distance from other people. Keep track of a sliding scale and try never to exceed ten over the course of a week.

Create bubbles of encounters. The people with whom one lives form a bubble, and it should be exclusive. Limit the size to no more than six people.
Nobody can belong to more than one bubble.

Wear a mask. If the risk of infection is average, at least two layers of cloth are to be used. If the risk is greater, more effective masks are indicated. The mask must cover the mouth and nose. There seems to be a preference to leave the nose uncovered. Think how you would feel if you were wheeled into the operating room and the staff wore masks that did not fit properly.

Until most of the population has been vaccinated, we must take every reasonable step to avoid spreading the virus. Asymptomatic carriers are the most dangerous in terms of continued spread. Healthy young people are more likely to party and socialize without masks and thereby spread the virus more widely.

We are social animals, and we are happiest when mixing with others. For the moment this is not possible, but we have invented tools and methods that make contact easier and more convenient. We will have to maximize our use of those tools until we have learned to live with this virus.

Priorities

By Diane Crane

One cannot hear the name Bernie Madoff without knowing his legacy. He was a greedy little man with no regret or remorse for his theft from so many people who entrusted him with their life savings. He left them stunned and poor. Their financial security vanished overnight.

Elie Wiesel was one of those people. Not only did Madoff rob him of his lifetime of savings, but Madoff depleted $15 million of the Wiesel Foundation for Humanity, an organization Wiesel founded to promote tolerance and equality. Mr. Wiesel's son was the first to get the news. He immediately called his parents to try to gently break it to them. Despite the shock, their innate response was that no one died. For sure, they had both seen worse. Money can be replaced or recovered, and they had seen more death than any person should suffer. Life can continue no matter how changed. But death is forever.

Covid has affected all of us, but those who have lost a loved one, a parent or a spouse or a child will endure a permanent and irreversible change. I am blessed not to know anyone who has died of the virus, but my heart is heavy for those who have. You cannot live in this world without hearing and seeing the stories of those who needlessly lost their lives. A father gone too soon. A husband taken away, dying alone with no one to hold his hand. Motherless children. Grandparents who will never bring joy to their grandchildren. And possibly the hardest to endure, the loss of a child.

There are thousands of doctors and nurses around the world who have worked tirelessly and selflessly for innumerable days and weeks that turn into months. In doing so, they have risked their own lives, and some have made the ultimate sacrifice. Those who continue to show up will tell you that they are broken. The stream of patients is never ending, overwhelming, devastating. The number of deaths is unfathomable. Bodies are stacked high in refrigerated trucks, waiting to be buried. Some are lined up in mass graves with not a last word to acknowledge their existence. The smell of death hangs heavy over the land.

An unexpected result of the virus is that we now all clearly see that we are not the "United

States" of America. It is undeniable that our country is polarized. Now we have Red states and Blue states. We have hoax supporters and non-believers. Despite the mounting number of deaths, many deny the existence and the severity of Covid and that those who do survive can be left with lifelong side effects of organ damage, severe fatigue, and vascular issues. Some experience brain damage, strokes or seizures.

I have no sympathy for those who claim their rights are being violated by being asked to wear a mask. It's a small price to pay to escape this virus and to protect others. Some balk at being deprived of having a beer at the bar or a meal at a crowded restaurant. I have little compassion for those who complain that they haven't seen their children or grandchildren in months. They should feel fortunate that they and their children and grandchildren are still breathing. They should feel blessed that those they love are not on a ventilator, many awaiting the inevitable fatal end of a life cut short.

Over the past years, I have often thought back to Elie Wiesel's reaction to the loss of his fortunes. It's a stark comment on priorities. It truly puts things in perspective. If we and our loved ones survive this pandemic, then whatever inconveniences we might experience along the way are a small and insignificant price to pay. We are the lucky ones.

One day, we will have conquered Covid 19. A vaccine is on the way. But the dead will never see that day. Those of us who survive will again live with the joy of being with friends, of hugging those we love and of going about our days as we once did. In the meantime, I can only feel sorrow for the thousands of those who are no longer with us and for the millions of those who loved them. And the saddest fact of all is the excruciating knowledge that it didn't have to be this way.

Finding Grace

By Janet Feldman

The loneliness overtook her gradually, like
a slow-moving but potentially destructive
weather system that the meteorologists had
been predicting for days, one to which people
either overreacted and later felt foolish, or
under-reacted and found themselves
shuddering on their rooftops holding
desperately created signs crying for help.
Grace had never been an over-reactor, and
loneliness was not something that could be
plotted and tracked on a radar screen. Social
isolation, the experts said, was as debilitating
and dangerous as any medical condition, and
Grace thought, "ridiculous!"

She had, after all, been somewhat of a loner
for decades. Long divorced, and estranged
from her only child, a daughter who had
married a Muslim and moved to some distant
country, Grace, after the disappointment of
these and other relationships, had relied upon
herself.

When they had divorced, due to Stan's
infidelity, Grace was able to capitalize on his

guilt and acquired sole ownership of the three well-established bakeries they had created together. Working as partners, they each were competent in all aspects of the business but divided the responsibilities, with Stan focusing on the financial and behind-the-scenes work, and Grace on the operational and employee aspects. She had grown the business to seven locations and developed a wholesale component as well.

After the pandemic began, Grace was forced to scale back on the wholesale end as her customers closed their restaurants, but the bakeries still did a swift carry-out business because good bread, chewy cookies and brownies are masterful comfort foods.

Grace had been too busy to think about relationships, and if she had been lonely, it had never occurred to her. The few times she had dated were unsatisfying, and she had found herself thinking about work and looking at her watch, rather than attempting to engage with her companions.

She had a few female connections from a businesswomen's group, but the social aspect of those meetings was never as interesting to her as the exchange of business ideas. She never participated in the casual talk about home and family life and excluded herself from plans for social activities.

As the pandemic stretched from weeks into months, sales at the bakeries declined. Money was tight in the lower middle-class neighborhoods. Bakery items had become a luxury, and even after Grace had reduced prices, bread was still cheaper at the supermarkets. She was forced to lay off some of her employees and close three of the shops. The remaining four bakeries were only open three days a week. The long-term employees did not need her assistance, and not wanting to let anyone else go, Grace made only a cursory visit to each location once a week.

For the first time in decades, Grace found herself with leisure time and no idea what to do with it. She had never been much of a reader, had no time to learn any crafts, and she began to watch far too much television, including old sit-coms and quiz shows she had never known existed. She also watched the news, every day hoping the announcement would come: "Pandemic over - everyone can go back to normal." Instead, the news became worse and increasingly ponderous to hear.

The mental health experts appeared regularly with their warnings about social isolation and their lists of remedies, nearly all of them including contact with other people. The realization for Grace was that she had no other people. She had neglected this important aspect of life, never reaching out, and even rejecting the overtures of others.

Not one to shy away from action, Grace began paying attention to what the specialists were saying. As a start, she searched on her computer for groups of people who had been divorced, and found several in her state, although location didn't really matter. She would not be seeing them in person, for now anyway, but should that day arise, better that they be nearby. Two groups of adults her age caught her attention, and before long she was actively engaged in Zoom meetings with perfect strangers. In fact, she mentally labeled one of the groups "Perfect Strangers," because of the commonality of being divorced, but also because of the safety of a lack of pressure for a stronger relationship. Grace was not ready to commit, even on Zoom.

Both groups had a format of choosing a topic for the weekly discussions, and as time passed, Grace found herself participating more and feeling that she was developing a connection to people in a new way. She was allowing others to hear her opinions on aspects of her life that she had never divulged.

No one judged her, at least not to her face. She was amazed at the openness and honesty of these strangers, who were now becoming friends, and whom she looked forward to meeting when safety was no longer a concern.

Grace also located a group that was seeking volunteers to make half a dozen phone calls a week to isolated seniors who had signed up for the free program. The purpose was to chat with the individuals, not to assess their medical conditions, but to talk about their lives and their interests, and most of all, to actively listen. After completing the orientation and training, Grace was able to comfortably speak with new people each week, giving them a short respite from their loneliness. She met fascinating people, intellectuals, high school dropouts, business owners like herself, and some extremely boring individuals. She learned that she had a knack for connecting with these people, many of whom wished to speak with her again, but the program was not designed to create attachments, and so the clients were rotated among the volunteers.

With her new listening and outreach skills, Grace felt confident enough to call several of the women from the business group and ask how they were managing. They may have been surprised to hear from her, but all were receptive to her suggestion that they meet on Zoom every two weeks to discuss not only current business concerns, but also to talk about the personal adjustments they had made during this challenging time. Grace offered to set up the Zoom site and was looking forward to talking to these women again, revealing more of herself, and finding another way to interact with people she had overlooked in the past.

Grace had not conquered her loneliness. She had yet to find a deep connection with anyone but realized how her own past behavior had alienated people. She considered contacting her daughter and trying to make amends but was not ready for what she predicted would be rejection. With the steps she had taken thus far, Grace believed herself to be on the right path. The suffocating weight was lifting, and she awoke each morning ready for something new.

Popsicles

By Elizabeth Mackey

I used to ration out the popsicles. A child would ask for a popsicle, and I'd have to think about it. Is this a good time for a popsicle? What other sweets has this child had today? What other sweets might this child encounter today? Do I need to save this popsicle in order to bribe someone to clean up the Legos later today? But I don't do this anymore.
Now I buy the Outshine no sugar added popsicles, and I buy three or four boxes at a time, and I let all the kids eat all the popsicles all the time, even right after breakfast. And I also eat all of the popsicles all of the time, even right after breakfast, or even instead of breakfast, with coffee. And we're all happy about all of the popsicles we're eating all of the time. And we all still really love all the popsicles, and we're not sick of them at all. We're only sad when the popsicles run out, which they do, kind of too often. And I guess, when we run out of the popsicles, and we have to stop being happy about getting to eat all of the popsicles all of the time, even right after breakfast, we realize that really, behind the

veneer of popsicle joy, we're also sad about, oh, say, everything else. Like we'd all rather be going to school, and to work, rather than eating popsicles all day.

My Pandemic

By Barbara Miller

The title is my pandemic because I want to tell you about how I am handling this nightmare. It is indeed a nightmare, however it is also our reality, dismal as it is. It will be over, and right now I do not see a light at the end of the tunnel quite yet, and that is the frustration.

When this lockdown started, I was grateful because I thought that the lockdown would keep the virus under control.Sadly that did not happen for a multiple of reasons. The middle of February there were stories on the news quite frequently about this horrible virus that was infecting and killing thousands of people in China and Italy. Our government did nothing to investigate and take precautions, and lo and behold, here comes the virus to America.

Now eight months later, we find out that the President knew in February that it was deadly. America heard a radio tape interview with the journalist, Mr. Woodward. On the tape we heard the President admit that the virus was treacherous, however he was not going to let the citizens of America know so that we would not be alarmed. Now, the president has blood on his hands. There are two hundred and sixty thousand deaths in America, and he is responsible for the major part of them.

We later found out that most of the spread of the virus was from Europe rather than China, however anyway it hit us really hard. Back to the middle of March when the lockdown started. My concerns, no, my worry was for my children and the rest of my family all living on the east coast where the virus was exploding. New York, New Jersey and Connecticut were inundated with the virus. Literally hundreds, no thousands, were diagnosed every day. There were daily briefings on television every morning that the Governor of New York would give us. He told us the unvarnished truth every day, and it was so hard to hear of the horror, however at least we knew what the truth was as ugly as it was. I watched glued to the news channels all day.

My concern was centered around my family and how they were protecting themselves from the virus. My twin granddaughters were in college in Pennsylvania, and their parents went immediately to get them because their school was closing, and they needed to be home. Once I heard that they were at home safely, I was relieved. My cousins contracted the virus.They are both pediatricians. They got the virus from a patient and were diagnosed very early and were able to isolate in different bedrooms at home and have since recovered.

I have my aunt that is one hundred and two and in a nursing home.The nursing home infections are soaring, and as of right now, she has been in her very small apartment since March. Aunt Mimi is the love of my life along with my Mom, and I ache to see her and hug her. I do not know that I will be able to do that. My pain of not being able to fly back east intensifies every day. I am lonely, however I am grateful at the same time that I have a safe place to be and that I am so lucky, luckier than a great many people. I discovered that the lockdown wasn't bad at first because I could relax knowing everyone I loved was healthy and compliant with the rules of the lockdown. I learned from the lockdown that I am a true introvert; I was always comfortable with being at home by myself, however this was truly the challenge that left no doubt in my mind.

March and April passed by, and on May first I was moving the pool furniture back to the pool area getting ready for summer that caused me to injure myself. I had a compression fracture on the bottom of my spine and had to leave everything and get into bed where I stayed for about seven weeks. The only time I left the house was when my amazing friends drove me to the doctor and the radiologist. I live by myself and having these amazing friends was a godsend. I did not feel the lockdown in as much as I couldn't walk or move without pain anyway. Lying in bed in pain most of the time, I had plenty of time to assess what was happening to our world, and it felt as if I had fallen asleep in one world and woke up in another.It seemed that quick.

We are facing a world we will have to get reacquainted with because I can see we will have a new normal. Right now, hugs and kisses can be a weapon.Visiting your parents is out of the question because the older generation is so vulnerable. I then had to admit that I was the older generation. All vacations, weddings, graduations, funerals or anything that requires you to be in a crowd of people can't happen for fear of spreading the virus and getting sick. I see that the worries of having enough of any and all things isn't quite as important right now. None of that is as important as making sure we have enough ventilators and oxygen and protective apparel for all of us. The reality of here and now and a light from the end of this tunnel was not even a flicker, mostly for the health care workers who are working tirelessly to help their patients.

I clearly remember the moment it hit me that this was real and terrifying all at once. I was driving to the gym as usual and the radio blasted that Broadway was closing. I had to pull over and come to terms that this is real and fear my mind and that the moment that I started my new reality that I am still living in. I turned the car around and started to accept this new reality. In May, because the numbers of infected people were coming down, in Nevada the restaurants and public venues were starting to open. We could finally get a haircut and get our nails done. This is not quite a necessary survival mode; it just felt really good. It was great to get out of the house for something, however I did not feel comfortable enough to go out to a restaurantor any large gathering.Fear of getting the virus was always considered before going out. I did go shopping with a mask and gloves. I was uncomfortable out of the house. I was appalled noticing that there are people that have learned nothing. They seem to feel that they don't have to comply with the rules that will benefit all. These people seemed just worried that we are taking away their rights. I saw a slogan on a car the other day and it said, "Mask it or casket". Is that really so hard to understand?

The lockdown started in mid-March. It has been so difficult, however I am very grateful living in my lovely house, having both refrigerators full and money to fill them if I want to. I am thinking about all those people that are standing in line for food to feed their children. I am trying to do whatever I can not in person because I am scared to go where there are a lot of people; however, I can donate money. Schools are closed and so are day care centers. What are these thousands of people going to do? A heroes act was passed by the government for the people who had to go on unemployment. These people received checks and additional money added to their unemployment checks. There was also a moratorium on evictions and mortgage payments. At least people would have a roof over their heads. In June, my husband died.He had Alzheimer's for five years. The difficulty in trying to plan a funeral or not was stressful to say the least. I passed on the funeral, and we had a cremation, and I decided to have a memorial when it would be safe. Our synagogue held a zoom memorial for him, and all our friends and family received some closure including myself.

Time really is flying, albeit every day seems so long. I am fortunate to have an amazing family and children except for the fact that they are all on the east coast, twenty-five hundred miles away. I am so very grateful to zoom and facetime. In the middle of the pandemic was a presidential election, it turned out fine for me, so I won't go into any political discussions at this time.

I think that when this nightmare is over, the next challenge will be difficult because there will be the new normal. I do not know how this will resolve; however, the younger generation will handle it. I have faith in our younger generation to handle it because it is going to be really hard and take time. I have no doubt that the children that we raised will create and flourish in the new normal. The older generations should be open and learn from them.

Covid Bubble

By Ritha Burroughs

Today Mother Nature chose to bless the town of LaVida with heavy rain. No one complained! The Nimbus clouds floated slowly into LaVida after a six-month absence to provide a break from the harsh dryness in the area.

I decided to seize this moment of tranquility and watched the downpour from the bay window. My Keurig was brewing a new holiday flavor, Candy Cane, and the scent of sweetness levitated throughout the house.

"Nana, here's your coffee." Ginny, my seventeen-year-old granddaughter, has been living with me since she was a baby. She is petite and has an olive-brown complexion. Her sister, Sheila, is two years younger, tall, slender, wavy hair, and a dark chocolate skin tone. Their mom deserted them when they were babies. I promised them that I would never do the same. I think they realize that now.

"Turn the tv on, Precious;" that's Ginny's nickname. And Sheila is Pumpkin because she was born on Halloween. How would you girls like to help me make some cinnamon rolls?

They both replied, "That sounds like fun."

"Let me watch the news, drink my coffee, and enjoy the rain for a minute."

Ginny shouted from the kitchen, "Nana, grandma is on the phone."

The girls call their great grandmother "grandma." She said they're talking about a new virus in China.

"Hi mama, if the virus is in China, you don't have to worry. That's on the other side of the world." My mom is ninety years old and very fragile.
She has lupus, partially blind, and uses a walker.
However, she is mentally very sharp.

"I'm not worried, honey. I just wanted to tell you about the latest news. What time are you coming over?"

My mom and brother live on the same side of the street, precisely four houses apart. The closeness makes it convenient for me to go every day to cook and clean. My brother, Jeff, is battling lung cancer and is going through radiation and chemo. He is too weak to help. My teaching job allows me the opportunity to have weekends and evenings free to assist them in any way.

On a windy afternoon in late January, the girls and I stopped by moms to cook catfish, fries, coleslaw, and some fried peach pies. Ginny came into the kitchen to peel the potatoes.

"Nana," The newscaster just announced that the United States has its first Coronavirus case.

"Sweetie, don't act like grandma. It's only one case. Our government is monitoring the situation. There is no need to worry. Tell everyone that dinner will be ready in fifteen minutes."

Looking back, I was very foolish to think that the Trump Administration would be concerned for the American people.

For the next couple of weeks in February, mama's concern about Coronavirus grew just like the number of cases in China and Europe. She worried needlessly for me, the family, the city, and the United States. I, on the other hand, thought nothing of the virus. My massive concerns focused on raising the kids, my mom's deteriorating health, and my brother's cancer. Why worry about something I have no control over.

On my morning walk, I stopped and said hello to my neighbor, Bob. After all the typical standard greetings, I asked him what he thought about the Coronavirus.

He looked at me seriously and replied, "I don't drink Corona beer, so I will not get the virus." That comment left me speechless; I smiled and continued my walk. I couldn't wait to get home to tell the kids about this.

They laughed and proceeded to correct me. "Nana, it is no longer called Coronavirus." The CDC calls it Covid 19."

"Well, thanks for correcting me. Ginny, you are just a wealth of knowledge like your grandma. You are a child; stop worrying about the Coronavirus. Excuse me; I meant to say Covid 19."

She rolled her eyes at me and strolled away.

Walking into the teacher's lounge the next day, I noticed a group of teachers huddled around the tv. Tracy looked at me and said, "They're talking about the virus being airborne, and we should wear a mask or some type of face covering." The bell rang, and we dispersed to our classrooms with solemn expressions on our faces.

At lunchtime, my mom called and told me to check on Jerry because the cases are rising in New York. Jerry resigned a couple of months ago from teaching to move back to the Bronx to help his mom. He had been my best friend for over twenty years and a part of our family.

As soon as the school bell rang, I dashed to search for an N95 mask at the hardware and paint store. It was even impossible to find blue medical/surgical masks at the pharmacy. The price on Amazon was sixty-five dollars for a box of fifty. Pre-pandemic price was ten bucks. Tonight, I will get out the sewing machine and design my own masks.

I cooked dinner early so I could join the family watching the news. It was heart-wrenching as they showed people on ventilators. And it was devastating to hear about hospitals experiencing a shortage of protective equipment. I found myself mesmerized by the evening news like the rest of my family. Each night that feeling of fear about this unknown virus increased, and how do I keep my family safe.

Later that evening, when I was alone, I called Jerry. I hope this time I could make a connection; I had tried for a couple of days but to no avail.

"Hello, Jerry!"

"Yes, this is he."

"Jerry, this is Rita. What's wrong?"

"My mom just died of Covid. I could not hold her in my arms. I could not tell her how much I loved her or thank her for everything she did for me. She died alone."

He started crying and hung up the phone before I had a chance to say a word. I called back, but no answer. My tears poured for him and his loss, but also, as I thought about the possibility of losing my mom.

The Pandemic was no longer far away but knocking at my door. While we had dinner, I told the family what had happened to Jerry's mom. There was complete silence and tears. After dinner, we turned on the tv, just in time to see the governor. He announced on tv that he was shutting down the state. He discussed the rationale and talked about what establishments would remain open.

My mother cried out, "Oh my God!" We all sat that in disbelief.

"What about my chemo and radiation treatments?" Jeff murmured.

I told him to call the doctor in the morning. I reminded him that essential businesses would remain open, and the cancer center falls under that category and not to worry.

"Do we have enough food and bottled water?" my mom inquired as she rocked steadily in the La-Z-Boy chair. "You can take my credit card and buy what you need for the house."

"That's not necessary, mama. The girls and I will make a list and go shopping in the morning."

On Saturday morning, I knocked on the girls' door and told them to get ready to go to the grocery store. I was shocked that I didn't have to go in and wake them up. They realized the severity of the situation and dashed into the kitchen in a record-breaking time of fifteen minutes.

We drove to the largest wholesaler, but the line extended around the building. I pulled out and headed for a smaller market. There was a line, but we were shopping within a half hour. I gave the girls a list and a cart, and I found one to purchase all the food and other necessities for my mom and brother. As I shopped, I thought about the homeless or people on a fixed income. What would they do? I thought about my mom's friends that lived alone.
What can I do to help them?

At that moment, Ginny interrupted my thought process as she hollered for me to hurry up. She said Sheila was in line to cash out. I had no idea the end of the line was at the meat counter. It took another thirty minutes to cash out. The girls and I did not complain; we had food. When we arrived home, I had to wipe all the food (boxes, meat, etc.) with alcohol wipes. Ginny sterilized the door handles and the light switches. Sheila cleaned the interior and exterior door handles and steering wheel. I washed the masks every night. Every time we return home, we follow that cleaning protocol.

Covid had redefined our world. Because of my mother's and brother's weak immune system, we had to be extra cautious. Our world consisted of my house and my mother's house. I taught my elementary Autism class on Google Meet as directed by the school district. Sheila and Ginny had their instruction on Zoom because they attended a charter school. There was no socialization for the girls because we were on lockdown. They found multiple ways to connect with their buddies using Google duo, Google hangout, Facetime, etc.

"Sheila, can you show me how to work Zoom?"

"Seriously, Nana, only old people use Zoom!"

"I didn't ask you what age group uses it. And I'm old. So, just show me because I need it for a class."

With Sheila and Ginny's computer skills, I became quite proficient in using the internet. Modern technology made life easy by ordering food online and having it delivered to the front door. The only time we left home was to pick up take-out food or drop Jeff off at the Cancer Center. Occasionally, I would drop food off at one of Mom's friend's homes. I missed school: colleagues, students, and my other activities. However, keeping everyone alive and safe was more important.

Around the first week of April, the phone rang; it was a New York area code, so I picked up quickly.
It was from Jerry.

"I have Covid, but I'm getting better."

You could hear him gasping for air. "I'm home." I went to the hospital, they gave me some meds and sent me home."

Another labored breath!

"Hi Rita, this is Anne; I'm staying with my brother to help him. I lost my mom, and I don't want to lose my brother. He is too weak to talk; will keep you posted on his condition."

All I could say was thank you. "Tell Jerry; we love him."

My family continued to live in our Covid bubble. It wasn't hard for my mother because she has not left her house in years. The girls are engaged in an online program with a Charter school. All social, music, and sports activities have been canceled. Jeff's chem and radiation treatments stopped for a while. A couple of weeks ago, he was so weak that he fell off the commode, and I had to call paramedics. My mom was crying, and he was almost in tears for fear he may get Covid if they take him to the hospital. The paramedics assured him he would be in a different unit than Covid patients. Of course, I could not visit him, and he was too weak to talk on the phone. It was tough to connect to the nurse's station to get updates. Finally, after several days, Jeff got discharged.

"Take me back to my Covid bubble," he said with a smile at least one foot wide.

Mom and the girls cried and hugged him for the longest. And he was so relieved to be Covid free when he left the hospital.

In April, I received a call from Jerry. His voice was no longer weak or gasping for air.

"I am coming back to LaVida. I lost my mother and now, my sister. Anne died last month. She nursed me back to health, and then she got Covid. I tried to take care of her, but her breathing was too erratic. The hospital admitted her; she died two days later. Alone. The nurse said she held her hand while she transitioned to heaven with my mom. Later, I found a letter in her bedroom. She must have known that she would not pull through. The message in the letter has helped me maintain my sanity. I'm leaving tomorrow to drive across the country to come home. There are too many painful memories here.

"I'm so sorry about Anne. She was a lovely person. You can quarantine in my guest bedroom upstairs for fourteen days."

"No, my friend Joe has a casita. It will be safer for me to quarantine there. I don't want to put anyone at risk. Love you, Rita, see you soon."

"Jerry, I have one request, call me every day when you are on the road, so I will know you're ok.
Love you too!"

In a way, I envied Jerry making the cross-country journey. However, I know the freedom of the road creates miles of anxiety. Covid dwelled in every part of America.

Month five of the Covid Pandemic, we were still in a lockdown. We had to cancel our family trip to Boston for June and the family reunion in July. This is the first time we didn't have a summer vacation. When you see the pain and suffering of Covid victims on tv or the food lines, a summer trip would be selfish, foolish, and possibly deadly.

The girls and I are amazed at people in the community who do not comply with wearing a mask and maintaining social distance. And millions passionately believe the virus is a hoax, and others like me realize the severity of the disease and faithfully follow the CDC guidelines.

We are learning more about the virus and the possibility of a vaccine by January. However, how many more Americans will die while we wait for the vaccine? The cases and death rates are increasing, and our country is divided in this Pandemic by politics.

As I sit on the front porch drinking my autoimmune herbal tea, the flowers are blooming, and the weather is beautiful. My family is alive, but the paranoia and the fight to keep the virus at bay continues to be a constant battle even though we are in our Covid Bubble. My mom continues to worry about me, the kids, Jeff, Jerry, LaVida and the United States. And I continue to worry too!

A Tale Sad but True

By Drue Kramer

As Michigan transplants five years ago, we cannot get enough of our new California homelife; not just our surroundings but, we gorged on CALIFORNIA. I am sure Californians know what I am talking about. Native gorging is celebrated as an artform out here. We are finding ways to incorporate sore knees and hips and canes with judicious travel plans. For instance, as eighty plus year old residents, our joy in hiking is pretty much limited to vicarious renditions of others' adventures. But our car takes us to wonderous coastlines, mountains, ranch country, parks, formal gardens, beautiful cities, lovely small art villages---the list goes on and on. The operative word here is 'car', our lifeline to the world.

In 2020, Covid-19 precautions have controlled our lives. No shopping; no visiting, only cabin favor. If there is any travel, it is in the safety of one's private car for an hour or two, just to get out of the house. That includes, of course, no dining inside restaurants meaning no access to 'necessary facilities' which put the screws to the 'pee patrol.'

Having not thoroughly thought through our first foray 'out' in the Covid era, we headed in the car to Benita a charming small artists village located somewhere at the end of the Bay. (For the life of me I cannot get my directions straight here. I cannot say the water and environs are this way and the mountains, opposite. Bay water is all around me, and the mountains are everywhere.) Nonetheless, we headed out for a Covid conscience day of people watching. I had packed a lunch, and indeed, we found an isolated bench facing a body of water hosting a marina. It was good to see the boats and the lines clanking the masts (longtime sailors, here). The afternoon was spent dreaming in the California sun and our water bottles, along with the PB & J and fruit I had packed, were long gone. Now came the sudden awareness that we were in serious need of a 'necessary' and Covid had closed everything up. The return home was an agonizing hour and a half run and a pledge to fix this problem.

In the past, when we traveled with our RV, all equipment and supplies traveled with us. There was a lesson here. Children were trained on a 'portable' Potty Chair. Surely, I could find some kind of folding apparatus that would serve my purpose in the car. Google answered my prayers.

I ordered something that folded up into a 16" pink square. It had an ingenious locking device that guaranteed stability, and although a bit smaller than I had envisioned, this would work. Two things were critical for its use. I had to be able to put my legs down as if sitting in a chair, and I had to be able to sit on it as discreetly as possible.

I tested it in the house on a dining room chair. Good and stable, it worked fine. Of course, it had to be tested in the car. We live in a condo complex with attached carports. At any moment, anyone might jump in their car to run an errand. Testing in the carport was not predictable and certainly not private. However, testing it in the condo guest parking space was an option. That parking was located completely away from the carports and condo entries. So, with confidence, I folded up my pink potty, moved the car around to the guest parking area and started my testing.

As I sat down on the potty chair, I found that the front seat tilted back a bit, losing the stability I needed and nearly fell out of the car getting up. I tried the middle/back seat. That was better. But the leg room was tight. And again, the cushy seats of the car made the potty wobble back and forth. I crawled over the front seat armrest to move the seat all the way forward and got stuck pulling my last leg over the armrest basically turning upside down to move the seat forward. Okay, maybe I could sit in the middle seat on the floor with the front seat forward—more space, more stability. I opened the car door and tried to sit on the floor. This took considerable adjusting and should have been a warning, but determination won the day, and I got myself squeezed between the front and back seats on the floor. Now, I was not able to move in any direction. I could not stand up. I could not pull myself up. I could not even roll up onto the back seat. I could not get out of the car! My only option was to squeeze my legs out from under me, slide like a caterpillar out of the open door, and collapse headlong onto the gravel of the parking space. As I stood up in defeat, I looked across the street to see a man seated on a bench watching this whole charade. HE WAVED AT ME. I 'discreetly' waved back and went inside.

The pink potty chair is stashed in my closet, unused, and I have been told that McDonald's has opened their restroom facilities up all over the country in recognition of Covid needs.

May 2020

A Day at A Time

By Marjorie A Bleam

Early in the morning,
When their feeder is back lit by the sunshine,
The hummingbirds look like fairies,
Or maybe even little angels.

The wind spinner - Dad calls it The Wheelie -
begins to turn.
And the shadows create designs on the cement
patio.
The birds are chittering and chirping and
singing. The mockingbird – we named him
Freddie – is actually yelling.

In the corner of the yard is a yellow bell bush.
I thought for months that it would die.
And now it has doubled in size, and it is
covered in bright yellow blossoms.
When the morning sun finds them, they glow
as brilliantly as neon.

The whole yard is alight and alive.
It's time to put down the paper
And the phone, and the worries.
The message is flashing right outside the patio
door: EVERY DAY IS A GIFT.

June 2020
More Sensitive Viewers

"And a warning," Judy says
"The images that you are about to see
May be disturbing to our younger or more
sensitive viewers."

I sip my wine.
Another refugee crisis, or a terrorist bombing,
Earthquake, fire or flood victims?
But no – Not this time.

The evening wears down.
I'm unable to think, to feel,
I can't concentrate to read.
I can't sleep. So in shock that
I can't even pray.

Slowly the reality sinks in.
I've just watched a murder
On the evening news.

September 2020
Just Stuff

My friend Marie is camping in her new condo, sleeping on an air mattress, eating out of her camping box, talking on the phone with me and watching YouTube on her iPod. She reports to her new office today, but her movers aren't scheduled for another week.

My daughter April's family has been living out of suitcases that are piled up in the hallway of their beautiful home - ready to be loaded if the next level evacuation order is issued.

I've been strolling through my house all weekend. I'm looking at the accumulation of fifty-five years with fresh eyes. There is nothing here that I can't live without. The birthday and Christmas gifts, the paintings and photographs, my pretty clothes, generations of memorabilia, Grandma's cast iron frying pan. It's not one thing – it's everything.

When I was twenty-five, we drove our two cars from Denver, Colorado to our new life in Las Vegas, Nevada. I'd never done anything like that before, and I didn't know. I brought all our clothes, and not so much as a paper cup. It was exciting for the two days that we stayed at the fancy Best Western on Fremont Street; and it was an adventure for the first three days in our brand-new apartment with a swimming pool.

But our moving van driver broke his ankle somewhere in Arizona. Calls to the company were useless – he hadn't reported in and they knew nothing of his whereabouts. Everything that I had so carefully packed was missing!

On the morning of the fourth day, I had a meltdown, a sobbing fit, because I didn't have my coffee pot.

It's so easy to say, "We're alive – the rest is just stuff that can be replaced."

That is, until it's YOUR stuff.

October 2020
Unstructured Doomscrolling

Atlantic Magazine – Advice for the last week
before the election:
"Bingeing on up-to-the-minute news is like
stress eating –
It's bloating our minds with unhealthy food
that will make us sick."

AOL Newsfeed
Apple Newsfeed,
Facebook & Messenger,
The Week
The Atlantic
Fox 5 Local
The Review Journal
Time Magazine.

You did this in the spring, too
When the Stay At Home first overwhelmed
you.
And you thought turning off the alerts would
solve the problem.

Are you looking now out of boredom?
Is it anxiety?
Depression?
No, that would be no interest!
Could that be better?

I think that THIS is the inability to reconcile
What is pouring into my mind
And what I am actually living.

And it's not for just another week,
Or another month.
I have to find a way to overcome this.
It IS an addiction.
My life is at stake.

December 2020
Best If Used By

In the times before the Covid pandemic
My days were marked by events.
Holidays and vacations, of course,
But also a sit down restaurant lunch
Or an afternoon of recreational shopping.

My days now are still pleasant – but
uneventful
And they are marked by the expiration dates
on the milk cartons.
The one in my refrigerator today says,
"Best if Used by Dec 29."

Time passes quickly according to these
reminders
And I sometimes feel that my time might be
running out

As fast as the milk that I pour on my breakfast
cereal.
I look into my mirror and I wonder -
What is MY 'Best if Used By' date?

Bummer Shopping Excursion

By Barbara Miller

It has been a long six months. That is how long it has been since the lockdown because of the coronavirus pandemic. Being a senior citizen, and that was very difficult to type, I am very careful about where I go when I leave the house. I Wear my mask and just go to the supermarket and then back home. I did discover that I really did not need to go clothes shopping after doing all my closets, as an activity. The other side of the coin is that I have nowhere to go.

Thank goodness for zoom. I get to see my family and friends, and I only have to have a small amount of makeup and a nice blouse or sweater and sweats. Zoom and facetime and live streaming have become a lifeline and a saving grace to my sanity. I don't mean to sound as if I am complaining because I am very grateful that I have a house and food in the refrigerator.

Saturday morning, one of my friends called and suggested that we take a drive to St. George, Utah. They have an outdoor strip shopping center that we usually go to once every summer. I agreed that it was a great idea, and I felt really upbeat about the plan. Bright and early, about ten thirty, we started out on the 215 to St. George. It was a beautiful day. Finally the temperature was under 3000 degrees. The traffic was a nice flow, and the conversation enjoyable. The hour and a half went fairly quickly. We got to St, George about twelve, and we started looking for a restaurant with an outdoor patio. There were not too many to pick from, so we stopped at a hamburger restaurant that was set up with social distancing outdoor tables. The burgers were very good; the fries were amazing, and the weather was lovely. Armed with a full stomach and the temptation of the first shopping adventure in months, we set out to the strip mall.

We got back in the car and set out a few blocks, planning to park in the middle of the stores so we could do half the stores. The approximate middle is Iron Mountain candy store. The parking lot was full however we did not see too many people walking around and the ones we saw not too many were carrying bags with their purchases. We parked and started walking and soon found out to our dismay that there were numerous empty stores, and almost all the brand name stores we usually shopped in were not there anymore. There were some new stores; however, they were not anything we were looking for. There used to be a kitchen store that we loved to shop in. It was a fun place, and it was a store that you could shop in for things that you could live without for the rest of your life.

The empty stores then hit me of the dire reality of our lives right now. Having been in lockdown and not shopping, I was sheltered from the reality that this is our new normal first hand. I am very aware now how far this country has been damaged by the pandemic. This was just a fairly small strip mall in St. George, Utah. America is huge, and hundreds if not thousands of small strip malls are in the same predicament. That leads to the reality of why, because of their closures, jobs have disappeared and people are not shopping. I am sure the people who have lost jobs are happy if they can provide food to their kids and pay rent.

We walked back to the car and decided to go into the Iron Mountain Candy store to shop, because when you are upset chocolate makes it better. I especially love it because they have a variety of sugar free candy that I really enjoy. Walking in we started having a conversation with the woman behind the counter. We talked about how sad it was that almost all of our favorite stores were no longer there. The woman responded that the mall was twenty-seven years old, and her shop was one of the first to open, and she is hoping that she can hang on until this nightmare is over. I mentioned the kitchen store,and she said that up until a few months ago there were four stores that were there since the opening twenty years ago. Hers is the last one standing. The woman said she cried when the kitchen store closed. We purchased our candy, and it was delicious and got back in the car and headed home feeling sad. We did not walk the other half of the strip mall.

I worry more for our country after seeing first hand how many Mom and Pop stores are closing. There has to be someone in the government in our country that will take the reins and acknowledge the pandemic and help to get our lives back on track. I know that we will not go back to living as we did before this pandemic started. There will be a new normal, and adjusting to it will be difficult, however it will be.

What Do You See When You Close Your Eyes?

By Janet Feldman

People, like most other creatures, thrive on routine and predictability. We plan our lives and make our decisions according to the structure that works best for us. We are sometimes open to change, but in general do not welcome it. Why is this? I would suggest it originates with our basic needs for security, stability and control. The pandemic has thrown chaos into our complacency, leaving us grappling to find a foothold and a structure where none exists. We can all remember the beginning, when people were hoarding toilet paper, an expression of a need to have control over an essential aspect of living. Supermarket shelves were lacking many foods and cleaning products, but toilet paper was not to be found. We have passed through that phase but are now once again scrambling like ants whose nest has been attacked by an unknown enemy. Each day brings accurate information, altered information and misinformation, like asteroids hurtling toward earth with the possibility of collision and damage to our already fragile structured lives. What is there that we can cling to for the reassurance that we all need? For some, it is religious faith; for some, it is a belief that our political leaders will direct us; for some, it is a trust in the scientists who are researching the virus and seeking vaccines and treatments; and for some, it is the strong desire to make their own decisions regardless of facts and regardless of the endangerment of others because they believe it is their right to do so. I think that we have more resources within ourselves. We need to look within and find our sense of self - what characteristics make us who we are? Are we compassionate, stubborn, agreeable, intellectual, athletic, artistic and so many more qualities which define us? A pandemic does not change our essential being, unless we allow it to. We may not have as many opportunities as we would like to express ourselves in ways that come naturally to us or to engage in our usual and pleasurable activities, but we are still the same as we were before chaos and tragedy struck us globally. We may, in fact, have more opportunities to express our humanity and concern for others through volunteering, through donating what we can, through reaching out to those less fortunate. Albert

Schweitzer said, "I have always held firmly to the thought that each one of us can do a little something to bring some portion of misery to an end." Perhaps not each and every one of us, but we have all seen and read news reports of people stepping up to share and help in whatever way they can, even those who themselves are suffering and have few resources. These people challenge us and remind us that amidst the darkness of the situation, there are still bright stars that shine. Close your eyes and what do you see? I see glowing sunsets and sunrises; I see fields of wildflowers swaying in gentle breezes; I see a placid ocean and an ocean filled with incredible life; I see snow-capped mountain ranges and forests and rivers and lakes, fall foliage and spring blossoms; I see the geological and biological diversity of the national parks; and I see smiles on the faces of those I love. What I know is that these things still exist and cannot be taken from me by this pandemic. Amidst all the uncertainties and fears, amidst the worst-case scenario warnings, these are the things that we can rely upon. Find a place that feeds your soul and spend some time there.

Blind Sided

By Diane Crane

Jimmy and me... we was just about raised up together. He lived over in the next holler. It wasn't very far. By the time I'd turned seven, I'd look out my window, and Jimmy'd be in my front yard, leanin' on the fence, callin' to me. In the summers, we'd be gone for hours. Sometimes we'd go to the spring up on the hill. It was always cooler there, and the water was cold as ice. In the winter, we'd go by the pond off Sutter Road, and if it was frozen, we'd slide on it until we got so cold our lips like near turned blue. One time we went down by the railroad tracks and built a fire pretendin' we was hobos. Back in those days, us kids could disappear for the whole day, and nobody'd think nothin' of it. It wasn't like now where mamas worried if their kids was safe.

Jimmy and me, we was best friends all the way through high school, and it was no surprise that after graduation, Jimmy asked daddy for my hand in marriage. He got a job working in the mines. Here in West Virginia, there are coal mining jobs and railroad jobs, and mostly that's all what people could do.

We grew up in the Amwell Baptist Church over on Old Route 60. My great granddaddy had donated the land back in the late 1800s. My people were all buried there, as were Jimmy's. Pastor Hines performed the wedding ceremony one Saturday evening, and people brought food and laid it out, and Mr. Kessler played the fiddle, and people did dance up a storm. It was a happy time.

Jimmy's daddy gave us a piece of land up over by Sims Mountain, and we built us a small, sweet little house. It weren't much, but Jimmy and me, we didn't need much. We were young, and truth be, we was crazy about each other. Over the years, we started a family, three boys and a girl. The boys help out with the land, and Sarah, well she collects the eggs and takes care of our two cows, Bessie and Martha. Everyone here plants a garden, and we grow beans and corn and cabbages and lettuce. When fall comes, Jimmy and me, we drive over to Ronceverte and buy bushels of tomatoes. I spend a full week cooking them into sauce and puttin' them up into jars that'll last us the whole winter.

We always make our way to church every Sunday. Now that Jimmy's daddy's passed, we stop there at the cemetery to pay our respects.

I hope his daddy knows what a good husband his son turned out.

Truth be, every morning when I kiss Jimmy goodbye as he's goin' off to the mines, I worry that he may not be comin' home that night. My uncle died in the New River Coalfield a while back. He was just 23. Men workin' in the mines... they come to expect a few deaths every year, but the times when there's a full-blown explosion, it's pretty bad. First you hear the ground rumblin' underneath you. Then, all the women drop whatever they was doin' and run to the mine, chasin' the clouds of smoke, just hopin' that their men will come out of it alive. When they don't, Pastor Hines is there for comfort. We're used to sadness 'round here.

So when we began hearin' 'bout this "pandemic thing," we didn't take much heed of it. From what I read in the Beckley Register, our President said it was a hoax. Then he said like a miracle it would go away. And Pastor Hines even preached from the pulpit that we had not to care about it. God was watchin' over us. People up north were wearin' masks and dyin' in hospitals, but we here in West Virginia... we was just fine.

Then one day after work, Jimmy came home with a fever. We thought maybe he was havin' the flu. He barely could muster the strength to shower and get the coal dust off him before he set off to bed. I made him some soup and hot tea, but he didn't have no appetite. Sometime in the night, I woke up to hear him strugglin' to breathe. I got up and rubbed some Vicks on his chest and sat with him 'til mornin'. I kept thinkin' the fever would break, but it just kept risin' up higher. I rubbed him down with alcohol and set one of my boys to fetch Doc Wilson, but Doc said he was tendin' to too many others. Seemed the flu was spreadin' everywhere.

Two days went by and Jimmy didn't get no better. He was so sick, I was fearin' for his life. Jimmy was a strong man, and I never seen him so sick. The Vicks didn't do no good, and I kept givin' him Tylenol every four hours, but the fever just wouldn't break. When he couldn't breathe no more, the boys and I got him in the car, and I made the hour drive to the hospital. I kept holdin' his hand, while keepin' the other on the steering wheel. He had to lean heavy on me as we made our way into the Emergency Room. There was people everywhere. Some was slumped in chairs in the waitin' room, and others was packed up in the hallways on gurneys. I just sat with Jimmy as he kept drifting off to sleep. Then he'd wake, strugglin' up to breath. Seemed like half the day had passed before they took him away from me. I sat there waitin' for word that he was gonna be alright, and I could take him home.

I never saw Jimmy again. They got him on a ventilator, and he never said another word. I never got to hold his hand and see him through it to the end. Neither me nor the children got to say our goodbyes. He was gone so fast. Wallace and Wallace took his body, but they was so behind with deaths that he weren't fit for a proper burial for over two week's time.

We laid Jimmy to rest in the Amwell Baptist Cemetery right next to his daddy. It was just me and the children and the reverend. I placed a flower on Jimmy's coffin, and each of us put a shovel of dirt over him until Mr. Jackson, the church sexton, could come by to cover him. I miss Jimmy more every day. With him gone, my happiness went with him. The children ask me why, and I can't give 'em no answer. Sometimes I hear Sarah cryin' in the night, but I can't go to comfort her. My sadness is too great. My tears hang in my eyes and fall down my cheeks every minute of the day.

Everyone said that virus wasn't gonna touch us. God was gonna protect us. Pastor

Hines even said so. How could it have went so wrong? Seems like every day now I hear about another friend or neighbor being taken off to the hospital, or worse. Jimmy and I... we shouda growed old together. We shouda bounced our grandbabies on our knees. It just ain't right. And all the while, I just keep thinkin' how I was placin' up all my worries in the coal mines, and I never gave no thought that the Lord woulda took him with a virus.

A Pandemic Rant

By Barbara Miller

It is mid December 2020, and the pandemic is surging out of control across the entire country. I am more frightened of the virus now than I was when it first started in January or February of this year. At that time, it was scary; however, there was a nationwide lockdown that I felt would resolve this nightmare virus. As time passed, it became clear to me that our government did not have a clue how to handle the virus, and the result was they totally screwed it up. No one knew anything about this, and our president knew it was a killer; however, didn't let the people of America know. He said he didn't want us to panic, but I think that his fear was that the nation was realizing how inept he was. I really feel as if he killed thousands of people.

Meanwhile, the virus was surging mainly on the east coast to the point that the hospitals were inundated with Covid patients, and our doctors and nurses were working night and day. We started seeing huge, refrigerated trucks outside of the hospitals holding the deceased bodies. The funeral parlors could not keep up with the burials. I was hungry for information from the president that was real news. Watching the idiotic content-free lies and evasive information at the news conferences that the president gave were infuriating. I have no medical background; however, I have common sense, and I knew that the president needed to step away and appoint someone to handle this situation. He needed to be quiet and let the scientists work at getting us safe.

The people of New York started going to their windows every evening at seven o'clock and applauding the medical staff of the hospitals. There were people banging on pots and pans, and some people were singing and playing music and in general making sure the medical staff knew how special and appreciated they were. Schools were closed from preschool through college, and then businesses came to a halt because of the lock down. Restaurants, Broadway, the Las Vegas strip, gyms and movie theaters were closed. Supermarkets shelves were wiped out. Getting toilet paper and paper towels was very hard along with cleaning supplies and hand sanitizer. Life literally came to a halt filled with fear of the disease.

Millions of people lost their jobs, and with that they also lost their health insurance in the raging pandemic. Confusion raged along with the virus because the information we were getting from the government was very confusing most of the time. The governor of New York was on television every morning with updates and reality checks. Governor Cuomo was for me my indicator of what really was going on. The president kept giving us mixed signals instead of scientific information. He literally told us that masks were not needed and keeping a six-foot distance from anyone was not really necessary after the doctors on his team told us that they were necessary. Masks turned out to be a huge deterrent along with washing your hands and staying at home.

The information on television was so depressing; however, I was glued to watching and feeling lonely and disconnected from the world. I started feeling sorry for myself a few days into this plague when I saw a middle-class family on a news show that was really down and out. The father was crying because he was so afraid of losing his home and not really having enough money for the next tuition payment for his son's college even though it would be virtual, he still had to pay the tuition. His daughter was in high school and doing online classes when she could because she had to share the computer with her brother. I was seeing many more of these stories every single day.

The Congress and Senate came up with the Heroes act. That was a bill that was passed to send $1200 dollar checks to people. A married couple received double that amount, and the unemployment checks received an extra $600 a week added to the checks. The virus started to decrease, and slowly some stay at home restrictions were taken away. Restaurants started to allow indoor seating at twenty-five to fifty percent capacity. Restaurants could reopen if they obeyed the safety rules of social distancing and customers were wearing masks. That helped restaurants to survive because they were still doing their takeout business as well. The situation was feeling like a B movie that you would possibly leave before the end because it was so ludicrous.

Those nightmares continued, and I realized that I was observing thousands and thousands of people getting sick and being hospitalized and so many of them dying. I also realized how blessed I am because I could afford not to go out because I am retired and did not have to endure losing my job or feeding my kids. It is so heartbreaking that people had to go to food lines that were thankfully opened everywhere. Memorial Day holiday saw thousands of people at the beach, not social distancing or wearing masks. Seven to ten days later, you guessed it, a spike in the number of cases. This was encouraged by the president of the United States. He was telling the people that not only was the virus a hoax but perhaps drinking bleach might kill the virus if you had contracted it. I cannot resolve in my mind that our elected officials allowed him to continue with the life-threatening rhetoric. I guess this is an issue for another day.

The extra money on the unemployment checks stopped at the beginning of July, and as of mid-December, nothing has been passed in the Senate to get some money into the hands of starving people, right here in America. It is a shame and an embarrassment. I don't understand the evil people who are running this country. How could they not know that the money that the unemployed should be getting is not going to be spent on new cars and or vacations or put in the bank. If indeed you want the economy to grow, the government needs to help out with the funds. These people want to feed their families and have a place to live. They will be giving it back into the economy, to the market for food and to pay their rent. How do these people who we elected to represent us look in the mirror? The good news is that two days ago the FDA approved a vaccine that will be given to health care workers and the elderly people who are in long term facilities, and that will start early this week. I am hoping that the Senate passes a bill to alleviate the pain of the unemployed as well. I am feeling that there is a light at the end of the tunnel, albeit right now it is just a flicker.

The Tiniest of Dangers

By Michael Pavesi

The drawings I've seen of the novel Coronavirus, obviously sourced from electron microscope imagery, remind me of the anti-submarine and anti-vessel mines used in World War II. Large spheres with magnetic detonators protruding from multiple points designed to obliterate anything ferrous coming close. With Covd-19, the arms standing out of the enemy attach to cells in the human body, wreaking comparable harm, sometimes fatal.

As the submariners and sailors of 80 years ago feared those mines, I fear this damnable virus. I have two of the major dangers: being over 65 and being a Type-2 Diabetic. When I think of my life in terms of overcoming adversity, I find no events comparable to surviving this disease-causing microbe.

Invisible, it's difficult to combat. Nothing to see. Nothing to feel. A phantom until for those unfortunate souls affected, it finds a pathway to mucosal membrane and attaches itself to cells and begins to multiply. Feeding on a body, sustenance exists in many organs upon which this virus thrives. The main target seems to be a victim's lungs. Slow asphyxia is the result. But as time passes, we observe many points of biological damage and a recovery that may take months, possibly years.

So, I gird my loins and decide I'm not going to let this invader harm me. I wear a mask whenever outside, not needing any governmentally sponsored requirement. I wash my hands when coming home from any outside venture. And I pretty much stay home. My routine sojourns to the outside world consist of food shopping and doctor's appointments.
I'm an adult.

Inside, I have genealogy projects keeping me busy. Lunch with my cat. A nap. Back to research. I seem to be more active than when I was working. Mind is still sharp. And I rather enjoy wearing pajamas all day. At night, thanks be to cable, Netflix, Amazon Prime and Disney+.

I occasionally join my partner in her tasks that require going out into the world. Or for a drive with no particular destination. Only recently have I ordered Chinese take-out, actually pick-up. Haven't eaten in a restaurant since last March. Kinda miss it, but my cooking skills have very adequately sufficed. Being retired, I don't have any income issues.

Between my partner and I, we are good money-wise. Bills are promptly paid. But I have enormous sympathy to those who are unemployed and trying to make it. I cannot comprehend how that must feel. How it must create enormous anxiety. The notion of not having food on the table is both frightening and incomprehensible. The idea of being evicted from my home is unimaginable.

I'll make it to the point where vaccine 2.0 will get shot into my arm. The population will eventually become herd immune to Covid. I'm concerned about mutations and if they'll be as fatal as the current model. Is this a merry-go-round of new numbers? Covid-20, -21, -22, ... Ad nauseum.

This is a wake-up call to humanity. Political boundaries have evaporated. Viruses float upon the air and strike in every land mass on this planet. Humans infect one another. Does it stop? What happened in 1918 and can we learn from that? Does my country take a scientifically based lead in combating the bug? Will there be international cooperation and sharing of information and resources? Is this a possible catalyst to a new world order?

No matter, foolishness is a regrettable part of this. The ridiculous notion that obeying a public health directive violated constitutional rights has killed and will continue to kill. Maybe this is a Darwinian culling out of the monstrously stupid? Our government reacted to this invasion with an ineptitude that defies understanding. The polarization of wearing a mask killed tens of thousands. And I find I have little sympathy for those who chose politics over common sense. It was posited that God would protect his lambs. Ask about the question of that defense of the recently departed.

I will be steadfast in following the right actions to protect myself and my loved ones. Multiple masks of varying colors and designed for the task. Antiseptic solutions and towelettes at the ready.
Hand washing when returning from the outside. Social distancing at a grocery store. Six feet. No crowding. Six feet.

A final rant: Covid-19 fatigue. How infantile. How it is that adults cannot immediately see the dangers of contact. The peril of breathing the effluence of pathogen-laden exhales. Potentially fatal contact with surfaces uncleansed of the virus. Grow up. Be an adult. Do what the experts are telling us.

Quarantine. Avoid social interaction. Wear a mask. Six feet, people, six feet. Or die.

I'll survive. But it does suck. And how will civilization fare?

Postponed Hugs

By Diane Crane

Life had changed a lot over the past year. Nora had been sequestered in her home for months. She had followed all the rules, ordering groceries and necessities online. Being in her eighties, she didn't venture out even for doctor appointments. She hadn't been face-to-face with another person since last winter, and now it was winter again. Christmas was nearing, but she had no motivation for dragging her artificial tree out from the garage. Why go through the trouble of decorating if none of her children or grandchildren would be there to see it?

The family always congregated at Nora's house. Her cookie baking efforts started the day after thanksgiving. Each day would be devoted to a particular type of cookie. There were thimble cookies and chocolate chip and sugar cookies and linzer tarts sprinkled white with powdered sugar. There were pretzel cookies dipped in chocolate and gingerbread men with buttons down their middles. Then, on the day before Christmas, she would take the plates piled high out of the freezer and place them all around. Nora needed all three leaves to extend her dining room table, and she brought extra chairs from the garage, carefully counting each one to be sure there was a place for everyone. The traditional Christmas ham was strategically centered on the crisp white tablecloth and springs of pine and holly berries accented the holiday place settings.

The family would come through the door, their arms laden with brightly colored packages, and the festivities would begin. There were hugs and exclamations of joy and little feet running to the tree to find presents tagged with their name. Nora's quiet little home would be turned into a cacophonous celebration while the radio played carols in the background.

But Christmas this year was cancelled. Covid reigned instead. It was more important to keep everyone safe, especially Nora, given her age. Phone calls would have to do for now. It was a decision made out of love so that there would be more Christmases, and more cookies and more Christmas dinners in the years to come. Trading future hugs for a broken tradition was the best, most selfless gift of all.

An Unusual Service

By Drue Kramer

Covid cheats a dignified memorial service. Nothing falls into the easy momentum of repeated practice. Everything is new.

My friend, Barb, lost her husband, George, in late December 2019 just before the Christmas holidays. It was a lonesome time of course as the adjustment to solitary life became a priority.

When a mate dies, you lose your footing. The regular order of life becomes a bewildering list of tasks lost in hazy days. Nothing gets done. Time passes. Pressures build, and then there is a blast through to time present, in Barb's case, the need to plan a memorial for George.

George did not die of Covid, but his widow and family were certainly victims of the "erratic planning" that the virus caused. His family was scattered throughout the country, and the sudden lock down in February was just the beginning of many obstacles they met planning the memorial for him. A Bostonian family member was caught in the "boxed-in" protocol imposed by Massachusetts, nobody in, nobody out. It was risky to fly. Many people in a confined space increased contagion. It was advised that only a small number of people should gather, 6-10 at most. Then the worst constraint of all, no gatherings were permitted inside (except for Florida's mega churches, "Unbelievable!"). In the meantime, Barbara was doing her best to cope with this life change and trying to keep myriad details in order.

An 'inkling' of value came from watching Television and the implausible machinations of Trump. Barb holds a doctorate in Political Science. The past four presidential years have been an epic dissecting laboratory worth hours of phone rants, emails, frustration. This highly intelligent woman was unable to keep luncheon dates straight but could accurately predict Trump's next act of 'in-your-face' arrogance or how the political climate of Bosnia would change in the next 6 months. Maybe overwhelming sadness can be soothed by overwhelming anger.

In May, at the urging of her family, Barb began to make the plans. Could the Unitarian Church handle a memorial service outside? Could she arrange for a "zoom" connection to be made available for those not able to attend? Would there be enough chairs for everyone? Would the weather hold? How could the audio/visual particulars be worked out? That was a singular worry for Barb.

Barb had chosen to hold the service under a huge sprawling tree standing solo in a grassy area of the church property. It had stood witness to many weddings, many Sunday School book readings, many years of children chasing around it, and once in a while, a solitary parishioner sitting quietly under it, gathering in the spirit of life. On a radiant clear day, one could see that magical mixture of shiny leather green leaves etched against an electric blue sky. George's Memorial Day was such a day.

The service went along nicely. The minister's sermon was clear and meaningful. A 'Boom Box' sitting on a chair in front of the congregation supplied quiet lovely background music.

Attending the memorial for George filled me with the warmth of home and family. By zooming the service, we could see old friends moving; see familiar surroundings, hear familiar voices and sounds. We were able to share an important intimate moment of life.

But then, as is often written, "the best laid plans....". There was some confusion about the use of the microphones, specifically which mic to use. There were two, both placed on chairs in front of the congregation to be used by anyone wishing to remember George in their own way. There was a lanyard mic which had an over-the-head cord just long enough to tangle with masks and eyeglasses and a very small mic somewhere at the end. The second one was a larger, more familiar hand-held mic.

Most people used the larger microphone, and sadly some of the memories were lost as people looked at the crowd and let the larger mic drift down to their belly button. Some people were suspicious of the itty-bitty lanyard mic and shouted the inevitable questions "Can you hear me? "and "Which mic is hot?" And, for some baffling reason, the music coming from the Boom Box turned itself louder or off during the service causing a daughter to scurry forth from time to time to adjust the volume.

Memorial services are unpredictable, always spontaneous, but we had heard many of the stories before, and we got to see everybody who spoke through the magic of Zoom. When there is no alternative, it is satisfactory.

Some would say that zooming is a vast improvement over long-distance calls, or letter writing, arts of a different time. Zooming is immediate, unequivocal, efficient, and alive.

Is it real? It certainly offers a veneer of real. I offer one argument: Hugs.

There is no substitute for holding a shaking friend, feeling her ice-cold hands and wet cheeks. Being a part of a moment, and viewing a moment, through zoom, feels like retrieving paper from the copy machine. It is only a record, not the dirty cups and crumpled napkins.

All in all, we congregated, memorializing George, describing our lives with him. I guess this was a way of reaffirming our own lives. "Yes, we remembered." "Yes, we will remember," reassuring ourselves that "Yes, George will be remembered."

Night shift

By Peter Philander

He stood at the window, looking down Broadway to the south, strangely empty on this Friday evening, except for the occasional ambulance with flashing lights and blaring siren. The noise was to reassure the patient to whom they were rushing, that help was on the way, more than to warn traffic in the way.

He put on scrubs that were fresh out of the dryer, smelling clean, like bleach, still warm. He donned his home-made mask, sewed by his mother and mailed to him, with cookies. He walked down the stairs, (walk down, ride up, the residents of the building had decided). On the sidewalk the air was cool and fresh. There was no smog or soot, a rare, good result of the city's lockdown. The storefronts were closed, the restaurants limited to take-out. The liquor store was doing a brisk business and a line had formed outside. Three people were allowed into the store at a time.

Six blocks passed rapidly under his feet and he encountered few people before he entered the hospital, eyes flitting around, looking at the benches where people usually sat waiting.

Today they were empty, anticipating a time when the virus was controlled, a time when people were allowed to wait there. The vague, undefined apprehension that seemed to have become a part of him, grew in his being as he went further into the building. The schedule was handwritten on a board behind the desk. He was to relieve Ann, who was nowhere in sight. They had come to work at this hospital together, on this rotation. Room three, he figured, that was where the most worrisome patient was and where she would be found.

He put on a mask as well as a plastic visor and pulled on the personal protective outfit, tugging the cover up to his chin. She was checking the patient, monitoring the pulse ox, the EKG, the blood pressure and the ventilator settings. Her shoulders slumped and the creases on her forehead were drawn in tiredness and concentration.

"Hi," he ventured.

She turned towards him, but he could see only the top part of her face, above the mask. He thought that there was a flash of relief in her eyes. "Is it time?

Have you really arrived?" She was spent.

There was a chair in the corner, a relic of an earlier time when visitors were still allowed in this room. He pulled it forward with a hooked foot and let her sit down. "How is this gentleman?" he asked her. "Tell me about your shift."

She sat, and he could tell that just sitting was enough for the moment. He listened to Mr. Adams' lungs and heart. He checked the latest numbers. He held his hand for a moment, figuring that even through rubber and plastic, there still needed to be the laying on of hands. As he moved around, he spoke quietly, commenting on his activity with a soft, low, soothing voice. He hoped that the murmur would penetrate through the woosh of the ventilator.

When he turned back to Ann, her head had slumped, and her eyes had closed. He woke her and gently steered her towards the changing rooms. "You're out of here," he urged her, and she went.

He returned to his four other patients, two of whom were a little more stable, and with whom he could be a little more relaxed. It was too large a patient load for this intensive kind of care, he realized, but there was no choice. This was the equivalent of monitoring a group of people who were under anesthesia. There really should be one anesthesiologist per patient.

He settled into a routine, walking between the beds and the rooms, adjusting here and there, monitoring, attending, waiting as the hours passed, as the clock ticked down. The hours of the small numbers were always stressful but now more so than at any other time. This was when human beings run low on the essence of life, when adrenaline levels ebb, when sleep is the only activity supported. He could readily fall into a self-pitying mood, but these were also the hours when he felt most valuable and nearly indispensable in the hospital.

Bob monitored Mr. Adams more closely as he needed ever higher pressures from his ventilator, and he developed some irregular heartbeats. An alarm went off, and the other caregivers on the floor came rushing into his area. Mr. Adams was coding. They went into their roles, one to do cardiac massage, one for ventilation and one to lead. Bob led the effort, but he felt distant and remote, as if he were far off, watching, waiting, observing, detached from this scene, by now familiar after having been repeated too many times. Fatigue penetrated into his very soul and he desperately clung to the small smidgen of humanity that he could extend to the man in the bed.

"All clear,"he called, and looked around as the others backed away. Then he delivered the electrical shock. There was a breathless pause, ventilation now done by hand, the machine disconnected. The EKG came back to a regular rhythm. He felt the carotid pulse. They exchanged a long, incredulous look.

"Let's turn him over, now that we're here," he requested. And it was easy with all of them working together.

The small miracle that his brain told him was likely to be a temporary reprieve, stayed with him for the rest of the shift, sustained him for the remaining hours. The new position, prone with his face to the side, seemed to help Mr. Adams. The ventilation pressure could be reduced. Bob worked on regaining his balance and his humanity by reminding himself at each bedside that this was somebody's mother, aunt, grandmother, sister, and he heard a little more cheer and energy in his voice as he spoke to his patients.

In the morning he walked back to the apartment, his earlier apprehension and anxiety discarded along with the protective layers, luxuriating in vision no longer impeded by a plastic guard that steamed up, bare skin feeling a soft breeze, at peace with the world. For that moment he felt that he had reached an accommodation with this tiny virus, our fellow traveler on this remarkable planet.

The Day After Duty

He woke in the early afternoon, his brain still busy with a dream of trying to turn a patient in a bed and not being able to do it. His cell phone was buzzing, and when he looked at the screen, he realized that the ringer was turned off. His mother had been calling on and off while he slept.

He answered her call and said "Hi, Mom," with as much energy as he could summon.

"Bobby, are you okay?" Her concern and worry was palpable in her voice.

He stretched out and yawned. "I'm fine, Mom. I was sleeping." He relaxed in his bed and listened to her fussing at him to keep her informed of his working hours and his coming and going. Her voice was soothing. But gradually he became aware of an underlying current of stress that was not usually there.

"How are you doing?" he asked, cutting across her monolog. There was a pause. He waited, knowing that she was blinking and was trying to figure out how to answer this interruption. "Are you sleeping enough?"

"Nobody is sleeping enough," came her reply, after some length.

He waited some more and finally asked "What are you worried about? Is it anything we can discuss?"

"Your brother called. He is worried about us and wants to be quite sure that we are not venturing out of the house," Bob heard her swallow, "ever," she said, with sad finality.

When she referred to his older brother, James as "your brother" it usually meant that she was upset with him. And James did tend to take a more pessimistic view of issues than he, Bob, did.

"We were sharing a meal with the neighbors once a week. He told us that is off. Then he started questioning your dad, and he got quite angry when he found out that he checks the mail every day. And he has cancelled our home delivery of The New York Times. You know how your dad is about the crossword puzzle." She sounded quite indignant.

"He just wants you to be safe," Bob ventured.

"There is safe, and there is ridiculous," she answered. "He wants to put us in a bubble and then he can come and look at us from a distance. Well, that's no way to live."

"How is Jim?" Bob asked, in an attempt to change the subject.

"He's very bossy, and very sure of himself, when it comes to our lives," came the reply. Bob heard the echoes of a familiar refrain. Arguments were common between his parents and their eldest child. The tug of war for family power resonated in his ears. It had been up to him to try and resolve these issues in the past and to come up with a solution that would allow them to get along.

"Let's start with the newspaper," he suggested.

"Yes. Your father wants the newspaper, and he does not care what your brother says. And I also miss it," she added, in a plaintive voice.

"Mom, cast your mind back to high school English classes." She was a retired teacher, and he appealed to that part of her. "Ray Bradbury wrote the relevant novel. And he said that books burn at 451 degrees Fahrenheit. That is more than 200 Celsius. Right?" He talked through the math. "Subtract 32 from 451 and that's 419. Then multiply by 5 and divide by 9 or divide by 2. That's easier. It comes out a little more than 210 degrees Celsius." He thought through his statement and decided that he had not made any errors. "Coronavirus is destroyed at 132 degrees centigrade after three to four minutes.

So, you can bake the newspaper after it is delivered."

"In English novels of a certain vintage the butler would iron the newspaper before presenting it to the lord of the manor. That would appeal to your father." She sounded quite cheerful. "I'll put it down next to his oatmeal." She chuckled. "How's your work and how is the city?"

"We saved somebody last night." He surprised himself with the energy and excitement in his voice." I had been keeping a close eye on him all through my shift, and when he coded, I was right there. I think that made all the difference."

"Tell me about him," she nudged.

"He's a fireman, and all of us worried about him because he's young, and he was just having such a hard time getting any air. After the code, we turned him prone, and he did much better. I could reduce his ventilator pressures, and every now and then he would breathe spontaneously. I think he's going to make it."

"I'm so pleased for him, and for you," she told him.

"The city is strange with the shelter in place order. It feels like a stage where the actors have gone home. The places where I enjoyed walking are now deserted. The bookstores are locked up. The people are few and far between. The energy has been sucked out of the place. "

"Are you finding some moments of happiness?" she asked.

"Last night, at work, and then when I walked home this morning, it felt welcoming. I'm going down to Riverside Park, and I'm hoping that there are some children playing on the swings and the slides." He sounded a little tentative, he thought, not sure that the children would be out, and if they were around, would they be practicing safe distances?

"Six feet away, they say," his mother reminded him.

"And you try to keep that distance with your neighbors," he told her. "Perhaps you can socialize outdoors."

"We'll try that," she told him as a goodbye.

An Afternoon Run

In the afternoon, he dressed in his running shorts and an old college t-shirt and headed out, going up the hill to West End Avenue and then down towards the river and the park. His gait was easy, and he felt light, floating along. There was little automobile traffic, and new leaves were on the trees. A group of runners passed him, and he noticed that they were spread out in a long line. Social distancing for joggers, he thought. He waited for the last one and fell in behind him, copying the rhythm of that man and of all the others being towed along.

He settled into the speed and pace of his fellows and let his mind wander. It felt like the days of high school, no competition and no stress, part of a team that ran for the sheer pleasure of it. Like a millipede with a thousand legs, they stepped widely around the occasional walker or baby carriage that got in their way, flowed like a stream and joined up again, without losing the cadence or the feel of the group. The leader, way off in the distance, stayed on the paths of the park and pulled them along, under the trees and then out into bright sunlight.

When he became aware of some fatigue in the muscles in his legs, contracting and relaxing, pushing him forward, up and then down inclines, he dropped out of the line. He stood, sipping his water, and he saw, with some surprise, that there were at least twenty more people who had joined after him. He walked away and sat on the grass in the shade of a tree.

His mind wandered into unfamiliar territory. Was this what he wanted out of life, this endless series of days with work and stress, analysis and problem solving? He had chosen academic courses and fields of study because it seemed obvious where he had to go and what he had to do as the next step in his life. There was always another challenge and another set of information to ingest and digest, process and master, incorporate into his thinking.

But this miniscule virus had stopped him and so many others. The processes with which he was becoming familiar had to be changed to cope with this newly recognized pathogen, and furthermore, it had changed the entire approach to patients. Previously, he was just learning to enjoy the slow ritual of getting to know a patient, establishing rapport, becoming familiar with their way of talking and relating. He was becoming accustomed to the vastly different approaches that each person used to cope with symptoms and disease.

In most encounters with patients, by the time the talking came to an end, the diagnosis was generally established. That was the lesson he was learning before this new, overwhelming infectious disease arrived. Now, there was no longer a slow unraveling of a mystery. The diagnosis was thrown in his face and the patient was often unable to communicate and arrived with no story and no background. He had to proceed to treatment and often resuscitation, without ever eliciting the history and doing the physical examination of this new person.

As he sat under the oak tree and relished the sunlight gently caressing his skin through the sparse canopy of early spring leaves, he contemplated the dominant new feeling that threatened to envelop him, when he first encountered a new patient in these days: Fear. Fear for the patient, for his own safety and fear for his co-workers.

In the face of disease and suffering he was used to sublimating concern and anxiety for himself beneath a metaphorical cloak of invincibility. The exuberance of youth had carried him through moments when he felt uncertain and anxious about his own well-being in the past. He had controlled the well-known student's temptation to identify symptoms and syndromes in his own body. But now those defenses were being challenged as never before. For the first time in his life, he experienced a profound, deep-seated and overwhelming understanding of risk to his person.

He had watched his share of scary movies, had ridden in cars driven inexpertly at high speed by novice drivers, gone for rides in amusement parks, and until now he thought that those thrills would prepare him for fear. But this was a terror induced by an invisible life form that had evolved to attack humanity at this time in the 21st century. He had learned a healthy appreciation for the sophistication and specificity of the medications that have been developed and that are used to counter the effects of disease on the body, but now he confronted situations where even the most powerful pharmacologic remedies were often inadequate and ineffectual. The methods that worked best, social isolation and avoiding carriers, are left over from a hundred years ago. His role, and that of all the other caregivers, is not that much different from the role of their predecessors in what medicine now regards as the primitive past.

The thought of returning to the hospital filled him with dread. He closed his eyes and let the fear grow inside him. Once he could contemplate the problem calmly, without being overwhelmed, he sat up, eyes wide open. And when he analyzed his shift at the hospital step by step, reviewing the personal protective gear, up to the visor and the surgical cap, he did not find a specific omission that put him at risk. He gradually controlled the fear with that stepwise analysis, and he fell into a restoring sleep. He awoke as the afternoon approached its end and he sat up, looking at the sunset through the trees. People were packing up, cajoling reluctant children to start the walk home. He had suppressed the anxiety to a distant, deeper place and he looked around calmly.

Back at the apartment, he ran the washer, made himself a dinner from left-over food, and after the clothes went in the dryer, he lay down and tried to go to sleep. But he was too restless and finally gave up and turned on his television. The images of talking heads and the disturbing, urgent voices were too much, and he rejected that, too.

He put on the scrubs, had a late-night snack and headed downstairs. It was early for him to go to the hospital, but he wanted human company and a human connection. The apartment building was quiet, asleep, the streets were deserted. He nodded at the security man at the hospital and thought of stopping to chat but decided against it. He was more than an hour early for the start of his shift when he went up to his floor.

He found Ann in room three, with Mr. Adams.

She looked up at him when he came into the room. "Hi, thanks for sending me home yesterday," she said.

"I was glad to do it."

"You're early, aren't you?" She was busy checking ventilator settings.

"I came early to talk to somebody. The rest of the world seems to be sleeping."

"I'm glad to see you." He wondered if her blue eyes sparkled a little more over the top of her mask and through the plastic shield. "He's much better. They plan to wean him off the ventilator and extubate him tomorrow."

Bob followed her to the next room, and they started working together, talking quietly." I went to the park to run," he told her.

"Do you run every day?" she asked. "I mean, are you a serious, committed runner?"

He chuckled. "No. I ran cross country in high schoo,l and now I do it when I can and when I'm stressed." He felt himself relax, letting go of stress.

Her eyes flicked up, looked at him for a long moment and then returned to her hands. "We can run together some time," she invited.

He looked at the top of her head, hidden under a surgical cap. "It is difficult to have a conversation with words and eyes only."

"Pretend that we are in the middle east and that's all you are allowed to see." She sounded playful.

"Leave me your phone number and we'll talk tomorrow. This is the end of this rotation for us. I'll be happy to move on." He watched her eyes, which moved up to his face. She winked at him. He winked back and they laughed together, quietly.

He later found her phone number written on the board where her name had been erased.

Quarantine

The wink was on his mind that morning, all through the small hours and then the hand-over of patients and the walk back to his place, through his sleep, with dreams of new people, new possessions, new beginnings. Along the way he decided that he should wait before he called her. She needed the luxury of waking up at her own time, when she had had enough sleep.

At a certain point, he started wondering if he had imagined it. Had she perhaps merely blinked, and he interpreted it the way he so enthusiastically wanted to see it. No, surely not. She had looked up, and they had made eye contact, and she had flirted with him in the only way that was available. The proof was in the phone number that he had entered into his phone's memory.

When his mother called him, by now a nearly daily ritual, she asked "You sound energized and a little excited. Did something nice happen to you?"

He thought for a moment and decided that he definitely did not want to tell her about the wink. She would read too much into it. "Probably post-call euphoria," he told her.

"Well, your father and I are happier. We've loosened the quarantine shackles a little bit, as you told me to do, and it is easier to live this way. We share the paper with the neighbors, and we bake it before we read it. So, it's twice-baked news at the end of the day."

Bob called Ann's number, and it rang a few times and went to an anonymous voicemail. His spirits sank as he left a message, wondering if she had left him a fake number. Surely not, he thought. There was a relationship and they had talked, and they shared patients and stress. Before he could go too far down that rabbit hole, she called him back.

They met on the street, and for a moment she tugged down her mask so that he could see her full face and her mouth in a smile. He felt a surge of happiness, a three-dimensional human being instead of a masked and gowned actress. He had seen Italian movies that featured scenes of fancy-dress balls where everybody was hiding in disguise. Perhaps this would turn out to be the morning after the masquerade, and they could get to know each other better.

They headed west to the park, jogging side by side until they ran into people, and at first, they alternated, taking turns leading as the other followed. They gave walkers a wide berth, but soon they slowed to a walk. There were too many people to keep trying to find a path and to maintain social distancing. And furthermore, a walking pace made conversation easier.

"How are you doing with your living space?" he asked her.

"Three of us share a fairly small apartment. It has been okay until now because of call and at least one of us has been gone most of the time. But today both of the others were there, and I sensed some tension. Nothing was said but I was happy to head out."

Bob tried to see if she was wearing a ring, but he didn't want to be too obvious about it. Also, it occurred to him that in these days of compulsive hand washing it might be that the presence or absence of a ring was not a reliable indicator of somebody's long term attachment.

"Today will be the end of our time here," she commented.

"Yes. We can take a few days off and then head back to our own program. This has been an extraordinary experience. You and I will be expected to present to the group about what we experienced here. We have to get together and plan that soon."

"Coming to help out sounded like a good idea, but now I'm not so sure. It has been a bear." She grimaced, and then her face relaxed as he cast a sideways glance. "Are we going to the river?"

"When I was a kid, we had a book about the lighthouse at the George Washington Bridge. I've never seen it, and I thought we could go and look."

"I don't remember that book, but it sounds nice."

"What was your childhood like?"

"I have a brother, James. He is four years older than I am, and he tested whatever limits my parents tried to impose. He's energetic and innovative, and he does not like boundaries. It must have been a real shock to him when I was born. My mother sometimes talks about how much he changed as he grew older. As a small child he was sweet and charming, and then he became argumentative and challenging. Now, when I think back on it, that shock may have propelled him to rebelling at them. I think I spent most of my time avoiding conflict or consoling them. In any event, he and I had totally different upbringings." He paused and then added "What about you? Are you an only child?"

"I have a brother who is older than I am. He was big into sports, and I paddled along behind him, trying to compete at the same games. Then I went into dance and gymnastics, and I went my own way for a long time, following my own path. But recently I have spent a lot of time alone with only my thoughts for company, and I thought about my childhood and those early years, and I feel much closer to him again."

They were approaching the river, going under the highway. They took a path that led them north, and soon they found a bench in the shade of a tree where they could sit facing the water. They settled at each end of the bench, six feet apart, he estimated. The bridge was away in the distance, to the north. "This virus has changed all sorts of things," he said to her, turning his head to look at her as she faced straight ahead, "Do you think that we can sit any closer or do we need to obey the corona rules that dictate this distancing?"

She turned to him and looked down at the ground. "I have never thought about where to sit down on a bench, before this. But you are right. The virus makes you constantly choose and adapt. I guess at this moment we should keep our distance. Then we can move closer if we become closer." She gave him a sweet smile.

They watched the sunset over New Jersey before they headed back to Broadway. "I would normally invite you to go out to dinner, but we can't do that. Would you like to cook together and then have dinner?" he invited her.

"I have to go home and change first. Do you have your own place?" She sounded almost incredulous.

"For the moment I'm there by myself. The guy from whom I rented the space, has gone home because of coronavirus. He works on Wall Street and can telecommute, so I'm alone. There's a grocery store around the corner, and we can go shopping."

He walked with her to the building where she shared an apartment.

"There's risk in almost everything we do. I don't see that spending time with you is that great of a risk. We have already shared patient care, and you are mostly self-quarantining, right?" She debated with herself.

"Yes. I've been alone here for three weeks, and I have not socialized with anybody else."

"Shall we meet at the grocery store on Broadway at 7?" she suggested.

Dinner Date

He was at the store a few minutes early and walked down the block towards her apartment building. He did not encounter her and walked back. She wasn't outside. He went into the store and strolled down the aisles, looking for her, but she wasn't there. By then she was fifteen minutes late and he walked back down the street to her building. She did not appear along the way, and since he did not know her apartment number, he could not use the buzzer. Back at the store, she still wasn't around. He called her, and the phone went to the message. He texted and decided to go ahead with the shopping.

He bought the fixings for a chef's salad and went back to his place. Once he had prepared dinner, he called and texted her again. There was still no answer. He was getting worried about her, and he walked back to her building. He asked at the bodega across the street if they had noticed anything unusual. The shopkeeper said no.

He walked back, rehashing the conversation from the afternoon. There was no hint of disagreement or rancor in his memory of the time they had spent together.

He concluded that something must have happened to detain her and to keep her busy.

He texted, yet again, but this time he wrote in more detail about his concern and worry. He added 911 at the end and at the beginning to indicate urgency.

This time she replied "I need to talk. Sorry about missing you earlier. Call me."

When he reached her, she sounded strained and distraught. "I've had a difficult conversation with my roommates."

"Did you ever get dinner?" he asked her, and she said no.

"Shall I bring you food?" he asked her.

"No. I really can't have you over here It is too difficult."

He walked towards her, and they met on the sidewalk, bumping elbows in greeting.

She walked back with him, her stride becoming more purposeful as they went, her arms swinging more freely, her gait lengthening.

He sat her down at the table with a plate of food and poured each of them a glass of wine. Between mouthfuls she told him the story.

"When I got back this afternoon, I found an envelope on the door, with my name on it. They put in a letter, asking me to call them when I got to my room. They wanted a zoom conference. They stayed in one room and had me talk to them on Zoom, as if we were having a business meeting. She stopped her description to comment to him, as an aside, "Not even a face-to-face conversation."

"Have you talked to them previously? Do you know each other?" he asked.

"I rented the room for a short term through the hospital. We've talked very briefly but didn't really exchange information other than phone numbers. They graduated from law school and are trying to make their way in the city but I'm not sure where they work or what they do."

She resumed: "They are fearful of Covid19, and they want me to self-quarantine, at the very least. All of this is conveyed in two dimensions, with light behind them so that their faces are caricatures. They would prefer it if I simply moved out, but they were not going to insist at this time. They had, somehow, not realized how much exposure I had to the corona virus until this evening." She stopped, and he could see the pain of the rejection on her face.

"Perhaps their parents talked to them. Perhaps they saw a program on television. Something happened to scare them. I argued and I tried to persuade them, but they were not moved." She sipped some wine. "They made me feel like a criminal, as if I had misled them and had been dishonest. They were firm, loud and insistent, like granite, unchanging and immutable."

He sat and listened to the tale of woe, making sympathetic noises. He turned on some music, Beethoven's violin concerto, as her words ran down. She let herself be soothed by the composition. She moved to the couch and pulled her feet up, stretching out with her head on a pillow. He put a blanket over her and when the concerto finished, she was asleep.

He dimmed the lights and the music stopped. He relaxed in his chair as his thoughts went to this situation. He and Ann were in a group of physicians completing a training program, and in this last year of their class, a request for help had come from somebody running a similar program in Manhattan. Their hospital was overwhelmed. Their staff was exhausted. The two of them had volunteered to spend time on this rotation.

After nearly three years of training, they thought they were prepared for anything, but this task had turned out to challenge them in ways they had not anticipated. The hours were long. The care that they provided was demanding, emotionally, physically and intellectually. Ann, this woman with whom he had trained, and who, during those three years, had sometimes bailed him out of deep water when clinical situations threatened to get the better of him, when he had to take care of more patients in the middle of the night than he could manage, had shown signs of flagging during the previous week. He had started going in earlier, giving her shorter spells at work. She had done the same for him in the past.

He remembered being in the emergency room on a Friday evening, caring for a young girl who had taken an overdose of acetaminophen. It was clear later that she was being melodramatic and thought that nothing bad could come from taking too many of those tablets. Of course, an overdose could lead to liver failure, and Bob was monitoring the administration of acetylcysteine to counteract the effect of the acetaminophen. A code came over his pager calling him to an in-patient for a cardiac arrest, and Ann, who happened to be in the hospital, responded to the code. By the time he had stabilized the young girl and had hurried to the other patient, he found Ann at the bedside. She sent him back to the ER.

They had collaborated a few times when one delivered a baby and the other looked after the newborn infant. There were many other occasions when they helped each other, but they had not developed any kind of personal relationship.

He knew her in her professional capacity, but in the past few days there had been the start of something more. They had both removed some of the barriers that stood between them and that dictated the way they behaved with each other.

On this day when she had let down her guard with him and they had started exploring friendship, her living situation fell apart. The apartment sharing was meant to be short-term and temporary. And the term had been about a week too short. He took himself to bed on that thought and with the hope that he would be able to kindle the little coals of intimacy that he had discerned.

The Morning After

Bob fell asleep late and woke in mid-morning in a quiet apartment. He was profoundly disappointed when he padded around until he found a note from Ann. "I am going to pack up. Thank you for a wonderful evening. We'll talk later." He was disappointed that she had left before he got up, but he decided that she was doing what she needed to do, solve her own problems and take charge of her life.

He checked the news feed on his phone and was soon absorbed by a story about hospitals and their economic woes during the Covid pandemic. The business model apparently was not doing well with the influx of really sick patients. Elective surgery was postponed, and other diseases seem to have diminished in incidence or severity during the viral infection.

He had been talking to a group in Chicago about starting work with them in July. He called his contact there and soon was engaged in a disquieting conversation. The position for which he had been considered was no longer available. As a matter of fact, the group's income had declined precipitously, and they were in the throes of reorganizing.

Bob called a different recruiter who had spoken to him at length a month earlier. He, too, had no good news. The sheltering in place to limit spread of the virus had caused widespread loss of business. Jobs had dried up. Insurance for health care had gone with the jobs, and the medical field that had invariably been strong during previous recessions, was now barren.

He thought of who else he needed to call about a job search and then decided that it would have to wait. His time in Manhattan was limited, and although the city was on lockdown, he could explore what was open.

On foot, the city was decidedly different from the one he had observed on previous visits, from a bus or a car, or the subway, for that matter. The walk to Central Park, along empty streets with only light traffic, was pleasant and diverting. The people he encountered were strolling slowly and he adjusted his pace to match them. Then he went south, along the west side of the street, the side with the buildings. He kept glancing at the park, but the avenue was also very pretty, with occasional flowering trees. At the Dakota he stopped, looking around, thinking of John Lennon. A wave of sadness came over him and left him feeling lonely, wishing that he had a companion with whom to share the day.

His phone buzzed. Ann: "Are you busy? Can we talk or meet up?"

He was elated to change direction to walk to her hotel on Broadway where they met on the street. Hotels in the city had set up accommodation for health care providers, and she planned to tap into that system.

"I woke up feeling like a new person. I ate cereal and had orange juice at your place, and I made some phone calls, including one to the hotel. "

They were walking back to Central Park. "When I got to the apartment this morning, the girls weren't there. They must have gone out or gone to work. I packed up and moved out. I probably looked funny walking down the street pulling my bag. At the hotel I showed them the ID from the hospital, and they were great. They didn't have a room at that time, but they were pretty sure that there would be one later in the day. They just about promised to keep one for me." The traumatized, unhappy woman of the day before was gone, replaced by this chatty, bubbly, energetic person.

'I walked down here across the street from the park, on the west side yet. I was reluctant to go into Central Park on my own, alone. Now I feel totally different, being with you. Let's go in there and explore," he told her.

They found quiet paths on this spectacularly beautiful May day with rhododendrons and azaleas in bloom, along with flowering trees, and finally settled on a bench, watching children clamber on rocks, finding finger and toeholds to go higher until they could stand tall, ruling their world. When hunger intervened, they walked to a deli on Amsterdam, called in an order and picked up the food at the door before returning to the park for a picnic.

The six feet distance between them shrank as the day went along, and when they left the park in the evening, and had to climb a low wall, she took his hand and let him help her.

"We have to give a talk about Covid19 when we get back," she reminded him.

"Yeah," he replied, "come back to my place. We'll see if we can do what we set out to do last night and perhaps this time we can have dinner."

"It seems like a long time ago." They held hands on the stroll from there on.

He glanced at her out of the corner of his eye. "Why don't we stop at your hotel. We can pick up your bag and you can stay at my place if you wish." She looked uncertain and uneasy. "You can sleep in my roommate's room," he added.

"If they still don't have a room for me," she decided to leave the decision to fate. And the room was not yet available.

Our Biome

They made a feast of a salad and sat and ate contentedly. The wine flowed, and they talked about their common ground, medicine.

"Microbiology has always been a bit of a stretch for me," he confided. "The idea of the invisible world living right around us is a concept with which I struggle. Lately I've listened to discussions of the human biome, the fact that we have many more bacteria living in us and on us and around us, than we have cells. And now there is discussion of the virome, the viruses that surround us."

"Perhaps it's because you're a man. That makes you think in terms that find small, unseen elements difficult to deal with. As a woman I learned long ago not to confront strength with strength. Women have to finesse their way through the world. If we want to move something, we slide it rather than pick it up and carry it." She sipped some of the wine.

"I attended a lecture at a national meeting a while back, one of those in a large lecture hall where every seat was filled. The speaker was introduced as a future Nobel prize winner in medicine, a man whose field was the ultimate in gazing at his own navel. He studied his own stool. That got quite a laugh from the audience. The featured speaker, a small, shy, bespectacled man of an older generation, then described the wealth of bacteria, the abundance of microflora that he encountered in 1 milliliter of stool from his own gut. We should not think of ourselves as masters of the universe but merely as the carriers and suppliers of those organisms, he said. That didn't get much of a laugh." He smiled at the memory. "That is where I was introduced to the idea of the biome. Each of us carries a personalized collection of bacteria and fungi around with us."

"I have incorporated that idea into my thinking. I visualize it as a shield, a protective field of life that surrounds us like a ghostly halo. Sometimes the organisms inside us can attack the body that nourishes them. That's what happens with appendicitis or cystitis. The germs get into the wrong place and cause an infection. We developed antibiotics to control them and to treat the infections, but we should be more careful and parsimonious in how we use the antibiotics. Used too freely, for the wrong infection or for too long, and we are attacking ourselves and our own protection." She stopped talking and returned to eating.

"So, we are cruising in a world filled with invisible, unseen, undetected organisms, and most of the time we are completely unaware of what we encounter?" He sounded incredulous. "And then, occasionally, we develop an infection that can be severe, and we become aware of that world that is not always benign but that can make us really sick and can kill us, for that matter."

"Think about evolution. Back at the beginning of life on earth, at least the life that we can detect, there were one-celled organisms. As that first cell developed, the first virus developed alongside it, or inside it. The cells kept developing and they coalesced and became ever more complex life forms. The viruses also kept evolving, but they never formed cell walls. They merely tagged along with the cellular types. After all these millennia, there are still two basic forms of life on our planet, cellular and non-cellular." She looked questioningly at him.

"Yes. You can divide the world that way, I guess. I always thought plants and animals were a good division. And then fish and land - faring. And somewhere along the way fungi and algae and bacteria. There are a lot of ways of dividing up the life forms on the planet. "He sounded a little petulant, even to himself.

"Fair enough," she said, "but in any event, evolution keeps going. And we humans have become the dominant life form on this planet. There are more of us than any other large animals, we are in more places, and we interfere with every other species of animal. The viruses that developed in the animals that we drive to extinction, are not simply going to disappear. They will find alternative hosts. And since we are the dominant species, we are, in all likelihood, the preferred hosts."

"Do you think that is how we got in this pickle?" He was growing tired of this discussion and started looking around for another activity.

She got up and started clearing the table. "Wasn't there a story of people eating bats in China? Perhaps they were the original hosts, and the virus spread to humans. But it doesn't matter. Now the world has to cope with the infection."

They went to the living room. He put on some music and dimmed the lights. She sat on the couch and pulled her feet off the floor, tucking her legs under her. She gave him a long, appraising look. "We need to talk," she said.

He sat down on the couch, near her. "I guess we do," he conceded.

"I held your hand today, and that felt like a very large step in our relating to each other. I don't know if you realized it, but that was the first time since we learned about coronavirus that I made physical contact with another human being without layers of protective equipment separating us."

"Was that pleasant or was it too much?" he asked, interested in how she would respond.

"For a moment it was almost overwhelming. The part of my brain that is terrified of this disease, wanted to scream and run away, but the part that wants human contact and closeness, that part welcomed the touch. And that part won." She sounded thoughtful, analyzing her emotions.

"The hand-holding only lasted as far as the hotel. Then suddenly you withdrew. You went off to find the registration desk and then the luggage storage people. I stood there wearing my mask, feeling in the way because people gave me a wide berth, and that's why I went outside and stood on the sidewalk to wait for you." He sounded a little hurt about being abandoned.

"Well, after I came out and found you, we walked up here, and we were back to giving each other space as the quarantine guidelines suggest because each of us had our hands full.

We were carrying and pulling things." There was a long pause.

She relaxed and stretched her legs and rested her foot on his thigh. He touched her toes and then explored the rest of her foot and ankle. She sighed, contentedly. He massaged the muscles and moved up to her calf. She pulled back, away from him.

"Not yet," she said. "It is too much in this place and this time. The virus is too near, the images are too strong, the primitive reflexes say flight or fight." Her voice was tense, the tension showed in her face as she stood up from the couch.

"I'm sorry," he said, placatingly. She stood still for a moment and then left the room, to go and wash her face. When she returned, she was calm.

"We will have to go very slowly," she said, "We have to really take our time. My emotions simply got too strained, and I had to get away." She shook her head. "There was no other choice."

"I thought I was going slowly," he said ruefully. "I'm sorry that I distressed you."

"My feelings are right on the surface. It is as if my nerve endings are exposed, and when they are rubbed the wrong way, they scream. I am not usually like this." She sat down, gingerly, away from him, in an armchair.

He looked at her, trying to understand what she was experiencing. He decided to talk about himself, in this situation. "I have gotten to know you in a personal, more intimate way over the past few days. Until then, I knew the professional, working you. And the more I know about you, the better I like you. I would like to see if we can move on from this moment, from this stress. I believe that it is possible that these feelings can grow and mature if we can create a gentle, more nurturing and supportive environment."

"I would like that," she said, "but it won't be possible to have that sort of mood here. I don't see how we can get closer in this city."

The Journey

He turned on the television in the morning and watched the news while eating cereal. She joined him at the table. He muted the sound when she sat down, and they watched images on the screen, chatting about breakfast choices. A commercial ended, and the picture switched to a policeman kneeling on a black man's neck. The victim was hand-cuffed and was rolled up against a police car, and he could not get away. They sat and watched in disbelieving silence. Finally, the policeman stood up when EMTs arrived in an ambulance and took the man away. Bob turned the sound on, long enough to establish that the picture was from a cell phone and had been taken in Minneapolis the previous day.

"That looked like a scene from an awful movie, set in a place that is falling apart," she said. "It is hard to imagine that it took place in the United States, this week."

He sought for words to answer her, but all he could come up with was, "I cannot believe it. There will be a reaction, a price to pay. Something must happen. This was a personal killing, and the image was as powerful as the planes crashing into the World Trade center.

How could that policeman behave that way? It was such unthinking, blatant cruelty exercised by one man on another."

"And the others did not stop him. Four of them were there, and they stood and watched, with no emotion, as if it were a completely normal situation."
She sounded distressed.

He put his arm around her shoulders, and she sat as close as they could get, waiting to let the emotions pass. Then they got up and started cleaning the apartment. They wanted to leave, to get away as if what they had seen was tied to that place and as if leaving the city would diminish the inhumanity of the act that they had witnessed.

He had driven, and she had flown to reach New York City. Flying felt infinitely more hazardous after their stint doing Covid patient care, and she was happy to join him in the car. Later, in the afternoon, they crossed George Washington bridge, and he caught a glimpse of the lighthouse down below where the captain of a boat would see it. A memory from his childhood echoed in his mind. He was in bed, and his mother was holding the book, and she pointed at the picture, smiling at him.

His eyes went back to the road and the cars. He felt more than heard the tires swishing on metal grids. Traffic was light, as if it were a holiday weekend when everybody was already at their destination. He watched the Manhattan skyline recede in the rear-view mirror, experiencing a surge of regret that he had not enjoyed this visit as much as he had the previous times. He wondered for a moment what he would find when next he came to the city. It was never the same from one visit to the next. One time his favorite restaurant had disappeared; the next time the club he frequented in the Village had closed, but this particular time had been radically different. He had felt a loss of vibrancy and vitality, a long sense of exhalation.

She was looking at her cell phone, tracking their progress, and flipping to points of interest along the way. She found a reference to the cliff face of the palisades that look down on the Hudson river, dark and impenetrable, like a defensive shield. Further on, her eyes found the turn-off to Fort Lee, made famous when it was closed as part of the payback in a political scheme.

"Road trips have a special place in my mind," he told her. "There is a sense of freedom and of unlimited potential. We can drive as far as we wish, until we get tired." She put away her phone and willed herself to enter the same place that he was describing.

They sat in their enclosed little cocoon as it carried them into the hinterland, sipping drinks, looking at the passing landscape, getting a sense of the drive and the afternoon. After a couple of hours, they stopped at a rest area, and she took over the driving.

"When are we due back at our program?" he asked her, as he checked his phone for messages.

"Why don't you call and talk to them? See what is expected of us," she said.

He found out that plans were fluid and that they were not really expected at a specific time. Clinics had been cancelled, elective surgery was suspended, fewer patients were showing up at the hospital and their classmates who were there mostly were occupied returning telephone calls, developing the new discipline of telemedicine. He spotted the opportunity for an impromptu, unplanned vacation and grabbed it, suggesting that they would do a presentation about Covid19 in a week or ten days' time. They would quarantine until then. That seemed to be acceptable, and he ended the call.

He turned to her in celebration and found her frowning, obviously troubled. Her hair was in a ponytail, pulled back from her face. Her hands, small and capable, gripped the steering wheel. She faced the road with concentration.

"What are you thinking about?" he asked.

"The killing on television. It was so awful," she said.

He turned on the radio and found a news station. Demonstrations were planned around the country. Commentators talked about a wave of unrest sweeping through cities large and small. They listened with rapt attention until that news item ended and then he turned off the radio.

"How could that policeman be so callous, unfeeling and sadistic. Were those characteristics not spotted during his hiring?" she asked, quietly.

"Nobody is completely evil or totally good. We are all, each of us, a combination of the two. That extends to every other human characteristic. Perhaps the tests that they use in selecting candidates for police school, tend to select out people with more of those traits," he replied.

Her blue eyes sought out his face for a moment before she turned back to the road. "You think that all of us have that in us?"

"I wouldn't put it quite that way," he said. "I think all humans tend to be tribal, and we

feel more comfortable when we meet up with people who resemble us more closely. That's what families are
about." He went quiet, thinking about what he had said.

They were headed west on the road across Pennsylvania, and he tilted his seat back until he was looking mostly at the sky, where high cumulus clouds skidded along. She turned the radio back on to NPR where there was a longer report of demonstrations starting across the country in response to George Floyd's killing. They listened for a while, and then she turned off the radio, saying to him, "I can only listen to those stories for so long, and then it becomes too much for me."

"I am just getting to the point where I can imagine the scene on the street, and I wonder if I would have interfered or would have tried to stop the killing. I am not sure what I would have done. Throw something at the policemen? Shout at them?"
He scowled at the windshield.

"I'm not sure that you could have done anything to stop it. That is the problem. Policemen have the authority and the power to use lethal force. When they step across the line, there is little that ordinary citizens can

do to interfere. Object strenuously enough and the same force might be applied to you."
She was half talking to herself.

They stopped in Pittsburgh for the night and watched television in their room while eating dinner. The news showed a march in the downtown in support of Black Lives Matter. The demonstrators were calm and peaceful; the police were watchful and did not interfere. The crowd was mixed with white, blacks and brown people intermingled.

They decided that they should stay another night and might join the demonstration the following day.

Meeting in the Morning

It was one of his occasional down days, one of those he knew only too well, when he had no energy and no drive, no ambition and a feeling that there might not be much of a reason for doing anything other than an internal sense of duty that would finally stir him. The anxiety and restlessness that usually triggered action got lost between the thought and beginning the doing. In the same way that he sometimes stood in a spot on the earth and had a feeling of infinite possibilities and endless potential, the opposite was now occurring.

What to do in that moment? Stay still and wait for it to pass? Anticipate the return of energy, or go out and seek it? Look for it wherever it may be hiding? But, of course, the way out really is inside oneself, and it is nearby, but not readily reached. Persuade the brain to switch over and become productive. This must be a minor, insignificant level of depression. In no way was this mood like major depression where there is no energy, not even a feeling of nothingness. That is simply a black hole into which one falls with no end in sight and no bottom.

What precipitated this loss of self-motivation? Was the cause insight into the fragility and transient nature of his motivations? Was it due to looking too closely at that which drives him to be who he is and to do what he does? Does it stand as a symbol, like the Greek myth of Icarus who flew too close to the sun and had his wings melt? Might it be the metaphor for looking too carefully and analytically at his own navel?

He stayed where he was, lying in the bed, curled on his side, facing a blank wall and the door. He heard the bathroom door open and thought of looking around, but his inertia was so profound that he did not manage even that small movement. The bed yielded, and he felt her climb in and wrap around him, spooning. His eyes opened wide, and he lifted his arm to make room for her to hug him.

"Good morning," she whispered in his ear. He reached back and pulled her closer.

He felt the warmth of her body and the smoothness of her skin. They stayed that way until every last vestige of his mood had been replaced by a sense of wonder and amazement. This woman, who he had started to think of as physically unapproachable and distant, was now as close to him as he had ever imagined a person could be. The emotional healing that she had worked on him felt like a blanket of soothing balm that he had never encountered before.

He moved slowly, taking infinite care not to disturb the mood of oneness between them, and he rolled over and hugged her. Her face was serene and confident. Her eyes sparkled, and he saw the beginnings of laugh lines around her nose and mouth.

They hugged each other, and gradually, tentatively, he started exploring the hills and valleys of her body, lingering with sensitive fingertips when he landed on a particularly pleasing place. With a small measure of surprise, he realized that she was reciprocating. He sighed in contentment. Each gave and received a sublime and penetrating pleasure that was increased and magnified by the sense of wonder that they could touch and could be close to each other.

The ultimate moment of coming together happened almost unexpectedly as a climax of sharing, and afterwards they relaxed together, drifting and savoring the nearness.

He became aware of a sense of contentment that was unfamiliar to him. He was close to her, so close that she felt like an extension of him, as if they had morphed into a conjoint being. He stretched languidly, and he looked at her face, and her expression was mellow, joy mixed with patience. Her mood was calm.

"Thank you," he said.

"We needed the right place and the right time. It erased my doubts and concerns." There was no tension in her tone, it was sharing and confident.

A Change in Plans

They stayed in that hotel for three days,
venturing out to get food and drink. Every day
they visited the same restaurant for take-out
meals and the same delicatessen for other fare.
They had to make reservations to use the pool,
and they found that early morning was their
best time there.

Mostly they talked. He had led a sheltered
life but also one in which he hid his feelings
and his concerns. She was a natural caregiver,
and he learned in that intense shared time
that he could speak widely and freely, and she
listened attentively and commented when she
felt it was appropriate.

She reciprocated by talking about her
experiences of success and of frustration in
trying to help others move ahead with their
lives. They learned about people who had been
important thus far or others who had been
unaware of the outsized role they nearly
played in their lives. As their confidence in
their mutual exchanges increased, their
physical closeness built upon that foundation.

When they finally checked out of the hotel,
they half expected that there would be some
acknowledgement of the experience they had

lived through in those four walls, but of course there was none. They merely provided financial information in
the form of a credit card and left.

He started driving, and they headed for the highway. The traffic was light, and there was lots of space around their car. Their mood was tranquil and relaxed.

"That was a wonderful vacation," he said to her. "We seemed to escape from Covid for a while, and I guess we now reenter the world."

"What are your plans for the next few months?" she asked him. "This is one of those times in life when decisions have to be made. Have you signed a contract with anyone?"

"You are right. I have to come up with something, and the reality is that the two places in which I was interested have withdrawn their offers." He pulled off the highway and stopped in a rest area. They set up a moveable feast on a picnic table.

Once they were settled, he resumed his musing. "My plans for after the residency have to change. The sort of family practice that I would like to establish or join, does not seem to be possible any longer."

She frowned at him, puzzled by his statement. "I was going to join a group, and they promised that they would guarantee me an income until my billing was enough to sustain me, as long as it was necessary. They figured on about a year before I was fully established."

"That is what has changed," he said. "Telemedicine has become a big factor. One can bill for it, but reimbursement is somewhat less than for an actual physical visit. Furthermore, patients are not coming to the office as frequently as they used to do. They are afraid of encountering the virus. In their eyes, sick people go to the doctor, and when the major disease is infectious, the waiting room becomes a dangerous place."

"You think that all practices are changing in this way? What you describe sounds awfully logical," she frowned.

"I was quite comfortable, choosing between two offers, but they have both been withdrawn. The two groups are no longer interested in hiring me. You should probably check with your prospective folks also."

She called, and he listened to her side of the conversation for a while, and as he noticed her stress level rise, he walked away to give her privacy. When he came back, she was thoughtful after her call.

Finally, she spoke to him. "It wasn't as clear cut as you described. They were still welcoming, but the terms are less generous. The guaranteed income is smaller, and the duration is more limited." She lapsed into silence. "In fact, I think that they would be quite happy if I were to cancel the contract."

"So, we are essentially in the same boat. We have to work out what to do. The big advantage we have is that we have spent a month working intensely with really sick Covid patients, and we have that experience. It was difficult and stressful, but we proved to ourselves that we can do it."

"Would you subject yourself to that same ordeal again, today?" she asked, sounding uncertain.

"I've had a wonderful few days, and I've recovered. Promise me a similar experience when I get time off, and yes, I would do it again. This is what we trained to do, and it is what we can do." He smiled at her.

"I don't think that I want to repeat that experience any time soon. It was pretty stressful," she told him.

"It would not be as difficult. We came in there on their terms, and they asked us to cover the time slots that were the most difficult. Nobody had any experience with the disease, and they were overwhelmed. You worked from four in the afternoon until midnight, and then I took over. We did that five days a week for four weeks. When you were off, you had to cope with room-mates who turned out to be unsupportive."

She shivered at the memory. "I cannot repeat that schedule."

He smiled reassuringly. "It won't be like that. What I have in mind is to sign on with a community hospital or a rural hospital. We'll provide hospital care rather than office care. At this time, the majority of the patients are going to be Covid patients, but few of them should require ICU care."

"It sounds so reasonable. How do we make this happen?" She looked uncertain.

"I've been talking to a recruiter who will let us know where the openings are and what the salaries are." He was getting enthusiastic about this idea as he talked. "The biggest issue that I see, is that if one were to do it alone, it would get very lonely. This last month in the city I would go home in the morning to an empty apartment. But I realized that existence was not my idea of ideal, and the morning when you slept on the couch and were gone when I got up, I felt quite abandoned. I think I could get used to the hours of work but not the solitary lifestyle."

She listened intently and when he stopped talking, she thought about what he had said. "We have had a wonderful vacation, and you are suggesting that we move on to a different phase of life. I need to think about how that will work."

He put his hand over hers and looked closely at her. "I've been living a funny, solitary sort of life with no real attachments other than to medicine for quite a few years. I am ready to commit to a long-term relationship with you. What we have now is more than I ever expected from another person. I have feelings for you that are new to m,e and when I thought that you had walked away in the city, that evening when I was planning dinner, I had a glimpse into the sort of loss that I could suffer. Since then, my feelings have grown more profound, and my attachment and desire to be with you has increased." He moved around the table and came to sit next to her, putting his arm around her and holding her.
"I love you," he told her.

When they stopped that evening, Ann went to get food, and he called his parents. His mother usually answered the phone, and he was used to talking to her with only the occasional conversation with his father, but this time he asked if both of them could participate. He then told them about Ann and his relationship. He talked at length about their training together, the three years they had been in the same program and that going to New York had brought them to one place and had created a situation where they functioned as a team with little emotional or physical support from anybody else. He talked about how they had developed a closeness and an intimacy that he had never felt with anybody else before, and also about how desolate he had felt when she wasn't there in the morning in New York, and how elated when they reconnected.

When he finally stopped talking, his father commented. "You fell in love. That's something that every parent hopes his child will experience. It's a wonderful emotion, and there is nothing else like it." Bob was silent for a moment, and his mother spoke up. "Congratulations. I am so very happy for you. Does she feel the same way about you?"

"That's what is really amazing. She does, I'm pretty sure." For a moment his confidence wavered but then he recovered, "Yes, she does."

"When is your graduation? Your program is nearly complete, isn't it?" his father asked.

"Yes, it is soon. We are driving back from New York together, and we're taking it slowly, making it into somewhat of a vacation. I figured I would call the two of you and introduce her before you actually meet."

"My goodness. This is tricky, isn't it." His mother sounded a little bothered.

"Can we call you in about two hours? We'll facetime, and that's as close as we can get right now."

When they were all together on the screen, there was a warmth of feeling that he had not anticipated. His mother, especially, was welcoming and receptive. She said that she had suspected that there might be a romantic aspect to his happiness when he was doing Covid care in the city. He listened to the conversation, and it sounded like people who had known each other for a long time. He relaxed, and let his mind wander so that he was pulled back to the conversation when he heard his name. His father was asking him for a comment.

He looked helplessly at Ann, who answered for both of them. "We'll talk about a party or a celebration when we have time. There is so much going on right at the moment that we will have to simply wait. For now, just having each other and building more familiarity seems to keep us quite busy enough."

After they hung up, he said to her "I do want to announce to the world that we are together, that this marvelous thing has happened to us. But I guess with Covid around, we can't do that."

She didn't answer and he dropped the subject, to think some more about it.

Graduation

They had both looked forward to a graduation celebration as the next step in their professional lives when they left the training ranks and assumed more responsibility and different roles. The virus changed the usual ritual. Nobody got together there was no dinner for a large group; no toasts were sealed with sips of champagne; much of the pomp and ceremony was done away with.

Instead, there was a zoom meeting with each attendee safely kept in a separate virtual box. The presentation about their corona experiences was part of a symposium for the entire hospital staff, and attendance far exceeded the number they would usually have expected. Bob and Ann had their opinions and experience elicited and analyzed because they were the only two who had a specific kind of intense, concentrated period of caring for patients who were severely sick with the virus. Their hospital had a few, isolated cases thus far, but there was a high level of anxiety about how to manage when they were inundated with large numbers of patients infected with the Coronavirus.

Ann described the turning of the firefighter patient, Mr. Adams, from supine, on his back, to prone, on his front, and his clinical improvement. She compared it to what was done in neonatal units. The two neonatologists in their ranks who cared for the smallest infants helped everybody understand the physiologic advantage of removing gravitational pressure of the heart and the mediastinum off the lungs and the improved air exchange that followed. Those quiet, reserved members of the staff were, for once, the focus of all attention when they suggested delaying the use of intubation but instead using positive airway pressure, as they did with premature babies. In that situation the toxicity of high doses of oxygen for prolonged periods was well known and that was the driving force behind the choice of ventilatory assistance.

The successful use of steroids had been reported in the United Kingdom, and there was extensive discussion of the timing of the administration of these agents. The pulmonologists pointed out that the regimen for treating respiratory infection in patients with COPD included antibiotics and steroids, so there was ready acceptance of the use of these drugs.

After the symposium had ended, the faculty and the residents moved to a smaller conference to discuss professional opportunities. Many of the job offers had dried up, and the graduating residents expressed great reluctance to accept positions where Covid care would be the dominant aspect. The conference ended on that unsatisfactory note.

Parental Advice

In the afternoon Bob received a call from his father. This was unusual, and he sat down with his phone to his ear, to listen carefully.

"Bob, are you familiar with the passage in Ecclesiastes: There is a time for everything and a season for everything under the heavens, there's a time to reap and a time to sow, a time to build and a time to break down."

"Yes, Dad. I know that passage. It is often quoted."

"Well, this virus has accelerated the occurrence of events and we humans must adjust to the change in the passage of time. I think that you should move faster with your union with Ann. Your mother and I watch the accumulation of cases and the number of deaths and none of us knows when and for whom the bell tolls. It would give us great comfort to know that your future with her is settled and secure." There was a pause and Bob reflected that his father sometimes thought out a conversational sequence and delivered it in totality. This was one of those occasions, he thought.

"Thanks for the advice, Dad. I'll think about it," he answered.

His father's voice was firmer and more assertive. "This isn't a moment when you should think about all aspects of the situation and then come to a conclusion. This is a time to act. We are, all of use, losing time to this virus and we don't know how much time we are losing or how rapidly the sand in the hourglass is running out."

"Has something happened to alarm you?" Bob asked.

"Nothing specific, just the quiet, immutable, inevitable accumulation of events and numbers related to the pandemic. It erodes one's sense of the predictable and when something good is delayed for no reason, one becomes anxious. There's an urgency about putting the appropriate things in place. And this is something that you should do. If there were a war and you had to go and fight in it, you would not delay making the home secure. And this is a biological war against humanity that was triggered by our messing with a particularly malignant virus. You need to secure your home front."

The Future

Their day was filled with activities, demands and needs, and there was no opportunity for a quiet conversation until late in the evening when they were sitting on the couch leaning against each other. "It was nice that they offered us jobs," he said. "Have you accepted the offer?"

"I wanted to talk about it. I do not want to do it if you are not there. I think we complement each other." She sat up straight and looked directly at him.

He held her hand and looked back at her. "You are really important to me. You have changed my life in a fundamental way. I cannot imagine going through life without you. I want to make this permanent."

"I love you. yes, yes, yes."

Pandemic Story

by Marjorie A Bleam

Wednesday Morning - February 3, 2040

Marji and Marie are having coffee together. Well, Marji is having coffee – Marie only drinks weak tea in the morning. They are each settled in at their kitchen counters with their wrist communicators on and their holographs hovering nearby. Marji can never resist teasing Marie about the weather in Vancouver. "I see that you have rain again today."

"I hate this weather!" she replies. "As soon as things settle down and we get a vaccine I'm coming back to Las Vegas for some sunshine."

Marji laughs; "You've been saying that for twenty years!"

"Did you get any sleep last night? He was really on a rant, wasn't he?"

"I had a dream about him. I dreamt that we figured out a way to send him gifts just by email and we flooded his office with cinnamon rolls. Isn't that just silly? I guess that I had them on my mind."

Marji holds up her fork. Marie looks down at Marji's plate. "Oh my gosh! Is that a Cinnaholic bun?"

"Yep – I found the recipe in an old article about Shark Tank. Do you remember when they had that little shop in Centennial Hills, and we'd drive over and get them fresh out of the oven?"

"Oh my gosh, Yes!" Can I have one?"

"I don't see why not. They're vegan so no milk or eggs. Do you have filament cartridges?"

"Yes, you know me – I'm always stocked."

Marji picks up her plate and walks back to her office. She sets the plate on the scanner and presses the number for Marie. It only takes a minute for the blue light to turn to green. As she walks back to the kitchen her notifications arrive: $4.50 royalty payment to Cinnaholic, $20.00 processing and delivery fee to Amazon. "Robbers", she thinks as she sits back down. She can hear Marie's 3D hum to life in the Vancouver kitchen. They resume their conversation.

"How did we ever get this old?" She muses.

"Speak for yourself, Boomer", laughs Marie. "I'm 15 years younger than you."

"Yes, but I never believed them; even back in the 20's when there were experts that said that some of us would beat the virus. At least, I never believed that I would be one. I'd have been happy to die in The Pandemic. I never wanted to live through all of this."

"Yeah, but you were smart." Marie doesn't say anything more, and Marji thinks back.

She can't remember exactly how the ideas had come to her. It wasn't a sudden revelation – more like a series of little thoughts that came together as she noticed things. The constant stream of information had morphed into the 'fake news phenomenon' and then the 'secret combinations' and conspiracy theories began to go public. There was the nagging unease about tracking and scanning and facial recognition. Her neighbors each talking about something that they had seen or heard and their growing anger over being 'lied to'. Maybe the final straw was when her AARP magazine published the websites of fact checkers so she could confirm what she was seeing and reading.

What was true back then? And how different were we from China, or Venezuela, or any of the many countries governed by those who 'needed to know' what its citizens were thinking and doing. Well, at least the U S Postal Service had still been functioning, and for a time an ordinary greeting card could arrive privately and inconspicuously in their mailboxes. Who knew if the officials were watching or listening, or even cared? It certainly seemed possible at the time.

So, thoughts and feelings were quietly shared with her family and trusted friends. As the questions of privacy were "resolved" and the nation's communities closed in upon themselves it helped to reach out to her loved ones and to be honest with them about her feelings. It had become a sort of game – checking their feelings and experiences against what they were seeing and hearing on the media. They were their own private fact checkers, and they could trust each other.

The few old Boomers, like herself, are the only ones who even remember a time without instant access to news and information, and what it was like to go somewhere, anywhere, without anyone knowing. Heck, she remembers when cell phones were first invented. She remembers what it was like before cell phones - being a teenager and driving across the country in her own car with only a coin for the pay phone and instructions to "Call collect when you get there."

And she also remembers the time when, years ago, she'd left her cell phone on the kitchen counter, and drove back from the grocery store parking lot to retrieve it and put it into her purse "In case something happens." She didn't realize it then, but the hook had already been set.

Their holograph wavers. "Hey, Marie, let me call you back – Tommy is calling." They both know that this is important. Tommy is her great grandson, currently serving. His calls are limited.

"Hi Grammy, how are you?"

Her relief is immediate, and she smiles, "How are you doing, Tommy?' Are you staying warm enough?"

He was wearing a short-sleeved shirt, so it seemed likely that he'd finally been transferred from that drafty and cold training center. He'd always worn his old hoodie before. She understood that he wasn't allowed to talk about his assignment, but he said that he was safe. Yet somehow, she felt that there was something more. What had prompted his call? And then Marie's words came back to her. "He was really on a rant last night, wasn't he?"

164

Funny how she had believed for years that the first one – Trump – had been the worst. Looking back now she had some ideas of her own about it. She had worked in finance, so she saw firsthand when the powerful on both sides had made their deals. The idea that the government's function was to protect its people was slowly eroded by lobbyists and corporations and special interests. The idea of common interest was equally eroded throughout the population by propaganda, and finally, outright fear and hatred. By 2016 it was a simple thing to exploit.

And the election of 2016 was, in her opinion, a race to the bottom. It wasn't just a fluke that the vote had come down to a balance of power mechanism known as the Electoral College – that had been manipulated through years of gerrymandering and segregation and polarization.

At first, she could rationalize that the election was a backlash to the globalization and unrelenting pace of change. He was, after all, just a TV personality. How much harm could he do? Turns out, quite a bit – but people were still working and had all their sports to watch. It was a time when the stock market was good, and the billionaires were at least pretending to be charitable. A time of

Bread and the uninterrupted Circuses of so many popular distractions.

And then there was 'The Pandemic' of 2020.There was opposition at first, but after a few years of so many people getting sick and dying the last of the social bonds were finally broken. Tracking became required and travel was banned for public safety. Social and family gatherings were strictly limited. She almost came to believe what she was told.

It wasn't so bad – from what she saw and heard the environment was improving. The shopping was excellent, and whatever she wanted was delivered right to her doorstep. The various news streams reinforced various opinions, including hers. And she had her Facetime and Zoom and YouTube and blogging and texting and video games. Many neighborhoods became more cohesive, including hers. Most families adjusted to the 'new normal.' Some (Marie included) held onto hope for a miracle vaccine. And the breakdown was not a Zombie Apocalypse. It was just a series of events that further polarized and isolated. In the end, the country just changed. By the late 2020's the government had full control of the media and the Covid tracking had morphed into the current model of quiet monitoring and intimidation that everyone has accepted as part of their daily lives. They are safe, but at what price? You still have your thoughts, of course, but every word and action is now subject to A I review. There are no such things as 'private spaces' anymore. No one today would ever engage in 'privacy'. Such risky behavior!

Marji suspects that there are others who, like her, are skeptical, but it is just too dangerous to try to connect. But maybe Tommy had connected with someone – a girl, perhaps. It's the 2040's after all, and his generation is coming into its own. She thinks that they are young and not so worried about staying safe.

She will wait. And watch. And listen more closely. Something is up. She reheats her coffee and takes another sip. "I may be crazy", she chuckles to herself, "but I'm not stupid."

Looking back

By the early 2030's the positive effects of the pandemic had been realized. Immigration law had been overhauled and was more equitable. Tracking everyone through Artificial Intelligence had a chilling effect on violence and there was almost no 'crime' anymore. The pandemic economy couldn't support the massive, industrialized prison system and all but the most violent of criminals had been offered rehabilitation. With over a million additional trained workers the major sectors of healthcare, technology and manufacturing flourished.

An enterprising employee at Burger King figured out how to put the base ingredients for 'Impossible Burgers' into his 3D printer filament cartridge. He printed Halloween treats for the neighborhood cats and dogs, but when his invention went viral the potential was recognized. It was not a huge leap to add flavor and color cartridges and to scale up the base ingredients (a plant-based mixture of carbohydrates and protein) for human consumption, and the new industry was born.

Factories were retooled as 3D printer manufacturers (every household HAD to have one) and countless providers of flavored filament cartridges flooded the market. Pretty soon microwaves were built right into the most popular kitchen models. But it was an executive at Amazon who connected the dots to the failing restaurant industry. Amazon devised a scheme to pay the restaurants a 'royalty' for their signature dishes and then built laboratories to create an exact duplication of the flavors. Your subscription now includes a restaurant dial up with transmission directly to your 3D. Any flavor cartridges needed for your order are delivered in less than 20 minutes. The fees are charged to your account automatically and are based upon the complexity of the recipes and the reputation of the restaurants. The quality and unimaginable convenience of this service quickly filled the pent-up demand. Nutritional elements were added to the base filaments and health food providers bought in to accommodate special diets. Scanners were repurposed so that, for a surcharge, you can transmit your own food to share with family and friends.

You still need to shop for fresh foods and dairy, and almost everybody still cooks at home at least part of the time. But the 3D is now as essential to the modern lifestyle as video screens.

The pandemic accelerated the consolidation of the American classes. The celebrity, political, and wealthy merged to become the Elites. They now control most aspects of life. But they have been smart enough to support and encourage the various working classes. There is no more racial inequality and very little poverty – only various degrees of prosperity among the Majority. During the late 2020's educational and various training programs flourished.

Not all of the 2030's was positive, but it's hard for Marji to remember when it all started. By the mid 2020's there was no separation between 'news' and 'media' but in all the media there was a big shift in everyone's attention to all aspects of mental health. The pandemic breaking of the social bonds had taken its toll – not to mention the ongoing isolation and lack of face-to-face human contact. That whole mask issue had quickly resolved into a fashion trend that continues to this day, but smiling is so essential to human wellbeing that the damage was irreparable.

It had actually become accepted – even trendy – to seek mental health treatment; most commonly for addiction, depression, and bi-polar disorders, but she'd overheard some talk about paranoia, too. Help seemed readily available.

But there were still plenty of guns and ammo and the occasional sound of a single gunshot soon crept into her consciousness.

Nobody at her level of society knew where it originated or how it had become available, but information about 'the fix' exploded onto the media. It was just so simple and easy. There began to be rumors about 'Fix It' parties involving whole families or neighborhoods or congregations.

The Artificial Intelligence designed to track and monitor everyone's safety began to fail. 'Freak Out' was actually the better term for it. Rumors were quashed, alternative facts presented, and communications of every kind were censored, but The Troubles raged like an inferno throughout the Majority. Even some of the Elite were caught up in the hysteria.

As the number of deaths grew the government became more desperate. Supply chains were disrupted, and it became essential to exert more control over the Majority. The final plan to save the country was an Elite consolidation of many old ideas and organizations combined into one all-encompassing organization: The Service. It is a mix of the Military and National Guard, the old Peace Corps, Scouting and Fraternal organizations, and even the older Depression Era Civilian Conservation Corps. Enrollment in The Service is required of every Majority child in the country upon his/her attainment of age 17.

Based upon the principle that "There is nothing more powerful than a motivated teenager", The Service has drafted, indoctrinated, and trained every American youth. There were no exceptions. Based upon talents and physical abilities, and – to be fair – in consideration of aptitudes and desires, each is trained and dispatched wherever and whenever they are needed. The Service covers every unmet need and all of the logistics required to achieve their assignments.

As the young people became more disciplined and engaged, 'The Troubles' were slowly replaced by 'The Service'. Service members are a focused corps, and they have their goals to achieve. At the end of their enrollment each is encouraged to remain in his/her field of service but can choose the city or community of his/her choice in which to work.
Most return to their families, but some do not.

And that's how the shift began. Marji recalls her father's stories about World War II and his military service. Her father was a child during The Great Depression and had lived all of his life on his family's farm. When he was drafted (at age 17) he had never traveled farther than 45 miles from his home.

By the time that he returned from the war her father had met and made friends with draftees from all over the country. He was exposed to different cultures and attitudes and foods. He traveled to bases in different parts of the country and was eventually stationed in Panama where he was exposed to yet another language and culture. He made lifelong friendships and returned to his family a changed man.

And so it is for the youth in The Service. The isolation of the pandemic years was dispelled when these kids, as Marji calls them, began to meet and train and work together. They were exposed to a wider world and it was clear to Marji that their attitudes were changing.

To be sure, their indoctrination ensured that there would be no squabbles with the Elite. They were solid Majority citizens. But still, there was a shift in their perceptions, in their willingness to rely upon the media, in their acceptance of the A I safety net.

Tommy

And now it is Tommy's turn to serve.
Tommy meets his companion Drew on their
first day at the Training Center. Both of their
last names begin with 'L' - middle of the
alphabet, middle of the que. They are finished
with their physicals and are waiting for their
immunizations when they start talking, and
something between them clicks.

They are exactly the same weight, and they
both have bright blue eyes, but everything else
about them is different. Drew is taller, so he
looks a little thinner. Tommy is stocky.
Except for the freckles, Drew's skin is so white
that he almost glows in the dark, and Tommy's
skin is a smooth brown. Drew has buzzed red
hair and Tommy's is dark brown and curly.
Tommy is from Oregon and Drew is from
Utah.

By the time that they are finished with
their shots they have covered the basics: their
gaming preferences, the virtual sports that
they follow, their hybrid educations, and their
hopes for their assignments in The Service.
Drew knows that he wants to be in the fire
fighters corp. A friend from his neighborhood
served on the Alaska tundra fires and he came

home to tell a lot of exciting stories. Tommy is undecided. He knows that he is good at organization – everyone in his family is – so he thinks that he might like working in one of the logistics offices. (In the end neither boy gets his wish, but fate may have taken a hand in that.)

They are separated into different groups for their aptitude tests, but Tommy can spot Drew's red hair in the group seated next door. But the time the testing and interviews are completed Tommy is so exhausted that he barely makes it through the dining hall and back to his barracks, and he doesn't see Drew again that day.

Drew had a Covid infection when he was just a baby. It is still a rare occurrence, even today. It left him with a heart murmur that disqualified him from the fire corp. But he had learned to read and write and speak Chinese at his private school, and THAT mattered to The Service.

Tommy learned his Spanish from his Grandmother Rose. It wasn't intentional on her part. A perceptive toddler like Tommy soon realized that when his Grandma Rose switched to Spanish, she was talking about him. One day while he was playing Rose overheard Tommy lecturing his toy dinosaur in Spanish and the jig was up. Spanish was added to Tommy's curriculum and reinforced in frequent conversations with his Grandma. His last words to her before she died were, "Adios abuela, te amo."

Tommy gets the highest score in his group on his aptitude test. Drew is second in his group. They are bilingual and they are smart. They are assigned to Communications.

As Tommy makes his way into the Communications line he sees Drew's red hair back in the line to his left. As he looks around, he notices that one of the Councilmen is taking notes and counting off heads as they check in. Tommy hangs back a bit as they move up to their assignment tables and watches to see how the companion teams are selected. It isn't hard to figure out if you know what you want. Each person in line is numbered one through six, and then the 'ones' were matched; and the 'two's'; and so on down the line. Amazingly, and to Drew's evident delight, he and Tommy are assigned as companions and given their directions to Indoctrination.

The Service Indoctrination is never discussed. Period. Marji has her own thoughts about it (the term 'brainwashing' comes to her mind), but when Tommy called her on his weekly day off, he seemed only a bit cold, but otherwise well and happy. Marji just had to have faith that whatever was happening would turn out OK. And it had. Tommy's call made it clear that he'd finished his Indoctrination and had moved on to his Service Training.

The former University of Las Vegas campus is now the Communications and Logistics Compound and Training Center for The Service. Las Vegas also remains a meeting place for Elites from all over the world. Tommy and Drew are at the epicenter. As future Communications Assets they are classified Need to Know. Their first classes are Modern History and World Geography.

The Logistics kids are learning about weather forecasting, procurement, scheduling, shipping, transportation, and every other aspect of the complexities to be addressed when The Service is moving and providing for the teams of specialists that must be quickly and confidentially located as needed. There is some overlap between their Logistics training and the Communications kids because they are allowed to socialize, and Tommy has always loved logistics.

The Communications kids are strictly limited in what they can divulge, but they're happy to mingle with their fellow trainees and learn from them. Communications is focused on monitoring and interpreting and advising The Service about emerging trends and any other information that might become an issue for the Elites. They are an expanded version of what used to be called the National Security Agency. Tommy thinks he's a spy and he takes to his training like a duck to water.

When the Elites consolidated their power, they began an initiative to change the common speech. Tommy is briefed on the old vocabulary, so he'll recognize any old words if they come across his channels.

Police and A I enforcers are now called, "Representatives". There are no more "Bosses" or "Leaders" - only a hierarchy of Councils and Committees. The old "Mother", "Father", and all the other nouns and nicknames that apply to familial relationships were too entrenched to be changed; but there are no more 'Marriages" – now 'Partnerships", and those who used to be your "Co-Workers" are now your "Companions". "Friends" are still "Friends" but everybody just refers to his or her acquaintances by first name. Last names are not usually spoken. Duplicates are numbered, as in, "I saw Tracey 2 and Bob 3 yesterday."

"Team Mate" is still appropriate for sports and groups of all kinds. Any term or exclamation that could be considered an insult is quickly censored from the media. "Comrade" was just too communist sounding to be used in the new vocabulary, and there is no longer a "President" or any "Politicians". Those titles are both too old fashioned for the country as it is now.

The Elite Consolidation was unopposed. People just got sick and tired of being deceived, and they turned their attention away from the government and to the media. It was a relief to be absolved of the messy process of voting – the candidates were so engineered that you didn't know who or what you were selecting anyway. The whole country gave a collective sigh when every Super Pac and Election Committee and Paid Political Advertisement was banned.

It's so much simpler today. In 2040 a representative from the government delivers an update to the media every evening. These are mostly entertaining and pass for what used to be "news". Sometimes there are rants but those are just added for excitement and no action is required of the Majority. Each morning when they check in with their devices, they are given the opportunity to like or dislike the prior evenings presentation. No further thought is necessary. Marji has to admit that even she responds to the daily poll. It gives everyone the illusion of control.

In Modern History Tommy learns that the current government is a modified version of the old Chinese model. By the end of the pandemic there was no need for any more posturing about Trade or I T or Human Rights issues. The Chinese and United States corporations, currencies and technology were already combined. The Consolidated Elite used the Troubles and then The Service to make their various arrangements for what was left of the two massive countries and economies. They operate now as one.

What used to be Mexico is now a collection of city states. During the pandemic the last of the failing government services were provided by the various cartels and they expanded accordingly. With any drug available anywhere without restriction, they are busy competing in research, development, and marketing and are meeting the global demand for more and more effective pharmaceuticals. There's still a heavier handed A I presence restricting the activities of their Majority, but that's just a cultural hangover from the old days. The city state model has moved into the failed countries of South America as well.

Iran somehow managed to reassert the Persian Empire. It now covers all of the old 'middle east' and as far to the northeast as India. Europe is realigned with the remaining countries on the African continent. There is no information about the Russians. Their borders have been closed since the 2020 pandemic and the Elites have moved on. It's assumed that their lack of communication and continuing isolation are the consequences of their failed government.

Overall, the Elites have done a good job of promoting peace and prosperity throughout the world. Immigration is now focused on the populations that have been displaced by the multitude of global warming events. Of course, it helps that there are not so many people as there used to be, but still, there's health care and food security and employment and entertainment for the Majority everywhere.

Marji thinks that it's unsustainable to have complete government secrecy for the Elites and no personal privacy for the Majority, but the worldwide Majority doesn't seem to mind. After what everyone's been through in the past 20 years it seems a fair exchange for their peace and prosperity.

Winners and Losers

Even before the pandemic there was a large contingent of Nomads in the United States – composed of everyone from the Elites in high end motorhomes to the disenfranchised who were living out of their cars and vans. Marji suspects that they are still out there, but Nomads from the Majority population certainly face a difficult life 'off the grid'. The Artificial Intelligence system works like this. All public spaces (that's everything beyond your personal living space) are monitored with facial and voice recognition. When you leave your personal living space your activities and contacts are monitored. This was very important for Covid tracking and mitigation, and for crime prevention, and is now widely accepted by the Majority.

Then, when The Troubles began in the early 30's, and for everyone's 'welfare', a check in system was initiated. Failure to check in at your assigned time triggered an immediate response from the A I – first by media, and then, if no response, by a home visit from a 'Counselor'. But "The Fix" was instantaneous, so no lives were saved by the check in system. Only bodies were recovered. As the situation got worse all media communications became subject to review - with surveillance triggered by key words. Any expressions of anger, frustration, or despair could come to the attention of the authorities. Everyone knew that their media was already monitored for commercial advertising purposes, so this really wasn't a great leap. And perhaps some lives were saved.

But now you must always be mindful of what you say. Any deviations from your normal routines might trigger additional A I monitoring. You make sure that your personal routines are unremarkable. These days everyone is either "hiding in plain sight", or, like the Nomads and the cruise ships, is completely "off the grid".

When the pandemic hit, and all the cruises were stopped Marji thought that it would be the end of the industry. But within a few years the ships had been reconfigured to accommodate smaller (mostly family) groups in separate quarters – each group with a private lounge and dining room. Activities are scheduled so that every group has the opportunity to swim, or use the spa, or go to a show or the casino at their appointed time. Of course, there is no docking in foreign ports, but the ships roam up and down the coastal waters of the United States – the Gulf of Mexico is especially desirable. And just as before, the Internet service is confined to a designated area with limited access and high usage fees. And no A I service after check in! It didn't take long for people to realize that their group could speak freely when they were in their quarters. Once underway passengers can relax and just be themselves for a short holiday break. The group cruise for a wedding, anniversary, memorial, or just as an opportunity to reconnect, is now advertised throughout the media and cruises are booked years in advance.

Stadiums and concert halls stand abandoned and useless in the 2040's – just as the old brick factories and manufacturing plants stood decaying and useless in the 2020's. The big venues – concert halls, stadiums and arenas - didn't survive. Event centers were just making a comeback when the Troubles arrived, and these massive buildings emptied for good. Sports are still popular, but either all virtual or played within closed groups. Music is actually more important than it was before. There are still Elite entertainers who publish their work on the media, and the Majority has rekindled a love for parlor music and front porch jams as well. The vast library of historical music is easily available so you can request any song that fits your mood, or fills your heart, or evokes a special memory.

Wednesday Afternoon -
February 3rd, 2040

It's February and Marji will be alone in her Las Vegas home until the family arrives to celebrate her birthday in May. She loves this time of year because the almond and flowering pear trees are already in bloom, and the spring weather will be mild. Penny wants to go outside and nibble the dandelions.

Marji had an older dog when the pandemic started – a dachshund named Doodles. Then she found a black poodle named Curly.

The world population has been so reduced by the pandemic and The Troubles that no one worries about overpopulation anymore. Young people are encouraged to have many children. But early on the new Elite calculated the enormous resources dedicated to the world's pet animal population – especially in the United States and Europe. As part of their efforts to allocate more resources to the Majority they waged a vicious campaign against pet animals. But the loss of so many pets was certainly a contributing factor to The Troubles, so now there is a compromise. Pet ownership is strictly limited to one per household.

After Curly died Marji decided that it was just too much trouble to apply for another dog, so she got a copper-colored Guinea pig. Penny is good company, and she loves to be petted. She has a nice cage with an exercise wheel, but she spends most of her time riding around the house in Marji's apron pocket. She knows when the grocery delivery arrives, and she squeals for her treats. And she especially likes to scamper around in the front yard on spring days when the grass is new and there's an occasional dandelion flower to munch.

Marji is carefully watching Penny explore the lawn. Her routine today is no different from every other early spring day, but she feels anxious. It's probably just the briefing from last night. Marie is right – in recent months the rants have become more and more frequent. But it's not just the media rants, or even Tommy's call this morning. Some little things have been creeping into her consciousness. One of the 3D cartridges she likes to order has been out of stock. There seem to be more planes in the sky. And last night, for just a minute, there was an interruption in her media.

Marji has just picked Penny up and put the little Guinea pig back in her apron pocket when an A I van turns the corner into her cul de sac. She moves back off her lawn and up to her front door as the van pulls into her driveway. There is a moment of panic as a man with bright red hair and a beautiful blond woman get out of the front seats; and then the side door slides open and there is Tommy!

As they approach her Tommy raises his hand to silence her greeting and then he slips a medic alert device over her head. At least it looks like an old Medic Alert device to her. It has a little blue LED light to show that it is on. They all step inside and THEN Tommy raises his arms and gives his Great Grammy Marji the best hug she's ever had. Tommy introduces her to his companion Drew, and then to the beautiful blond. Her name is Diane and Marji can tell right away that there is something special about her.

There is some excited chatter at first, but Tommy is anxious to get down to business. After they are all set up at the kitchen counter with tea and cookies, he begins his explanation.

"I'm sorry that I couldn't say anything this morning, but we needed to do a final sync with your A I before we showed up." Marji notes that Tommy, Drew and Diane are also wearing Medic Alerts. He laughs. "Diane got these for us. They are first generation jamming devices for media and A I. The Elite have been using them since the beginning, but this model is obsolete now – they all wear theirs as micro inserts in their jewelry. But these old ones still operate, so we can speak freely. From now on just push your 'Medic Alert' button when we're talking.

Grammy, I'm afraid that there's more trouble coming. Drew and I have been monitoring their communications – and The Elite Class is collapsing. The older Elites who lived through the pandemic and took control have been using genetic engineering to stay alive – but the technology can only go so far, and now they have started to die off. These are the men and women who, in spite of their mistakes, have managed to use their fortunes and influence to establish and maintain a secure Majority. They understood that the Elite Class is dependent upon a stable working Majority. Their children and grandchildren could not care less. They feel entitled to the benefits of the Elite lifestyle with no responsibility for the system that supports it. Their excesses make the Roman Empire look like a Puritan Church meeting, and with their elders gone they have been jetting in and out of Las Vegas for secret meetings - seeking even more wealth and power for themselves.

We think that when their world disintegrates, they will take the Majority down with them.

Drew and I met Diane at the Training Center and we have been working together. She's a wiz at logistics and she has access to the entire database and the equipment storage. Diane found an abandoned warehouse just outside of Fairbanks, Alaska. The Service left it there in case there were any more tundra fires, and it's still stocked with equipment – shelters, pumps and solar generators, tools of every kind, electric off road vehicles, even a completely stocked field hospital. We have requested assignments in Alaska, and we will be moving to Anchorage when we graduate from the Training Center. Our plan is to keep gathering the resources that we'll need, and when we are ready, we will move everyone to a place where we can start over."

Marji has tears rolling down her cheeks. She has never felt more exhausted and overwhelmed. "What do you need from me, Tommy?"

"Grammy, do you still have the books?"

She has a flashback to 2019, when she helped Marie pack for that first move to Vancouver. They were in Marie's office and Marie's daughter was packing the books for donation. "You don't need these, Mother! Everything is online and they are too heavy to move."

Marji walks Tommy and Drew and Diane back to her little office. She's been subject to much ridicule over the years, but yes – she still has the books. Not the novels, of course – it would have been impossible to keep all of those – but she's kept the reference books. She has the Compton's Encyclopedia and Webster's Dictionary from her high school days. She has the Life series: Nature, Science, and World. She has the Funk & Wagnalls.

Young Students Encyclopedia and the Bookshelf for Boys & Girls with the best classic stories ever written.

Oh yes, she still has the books.

Now it's Tommy's turn to cry. "Oh Grammy, you don't know what this means to us! We will be starting over without any media. These books will be the foundation of our children's education. They are our only resource to early history, science, literature and religion. Can we take them with us?"

Empty boxes are removed from the van and carefully packed. Diane catalogs and labels each box. They will be shipped in small secure batches to the warehouse in Alaska.

As the last boxes are loaded Tommy turns to his Grammy and hands her a small package. Inside the package is a silver charm with a strange symbol. "Wear this, Grammy. It shows that you are one of us. Stay Safe, Stay Well, and Watch. I love you."
The van door slides shut, and Tommy is gone.

Planning

Over the next few weeks Marji and Tommy use their "medic-alerts' to talk and to plan. "Drew found the file", explained Tommy. "It was a briefing from the Chinese Elites and it explained what has happened in Russia over the past 20 years.

You probably remember, Grammy, that when the Pandemic hit Russia was already on shaky grounds, both politically and economically. The power and corruption of then President Putin and the oligarchs was coming under increasing scrutiny by the Russian people, and there were even some political opponents. The Chinese file tells us that the Russian's vaccine for the Coronavirus was ineffective, but the government hid that from their citizens and distributed the doses anyway – probably in an attempt to retain their power and to get ahead of the anticipated economic recovery.

When the Russians were overwhelmed with Coronavirus sickness and death the truth leaked out, and the people's outrage was uncontrollable. There was a revolution to overthrow the government. The upheaval and fighting in Russia continued into the 2030's. But during this time, we were distracted by our own upheavals: the collapse of so many governments and consolidation of power by the Elites, their rebuilding of the Majority Classes and our economies, and, of course, The Troubles. The Elites knew what was happening in Russia, but the last thing that they wanted was a Russian Revolution inspiring the rest of the world. Because they control the media, they made certain that everything happening in Russia remained secret. And Russia was left on its own.

The wealthy and powerful maintained their hold on Western Russia and the Balkan states, but in 2035 the area east of the Volga River and north of Kazakhstan and Mongolia was granted independence. All of the Siberian region is a free country now, and Kazakhstan and Mongolia have aligned themselves with their northern neighbor. New Siberia has the greatest amount of land and the smallest number of people of any country in the world. They need a vibrant population to survive, so last year the people of New Siberia approved immigration to their country.

The New Siberian government is small, and the country is basically an open frontier. They are looking for self-sufficient groups who will be able to colonize and help the country grow according to the vision that the people have set for themselves. There is freedom of speech and religion, and no ethnic discrimination (which is a big thing for the former Russians). Men and women have equal rights, but it is a matriarchal society. And, most importantly, there is no internet – absolutely no media. The government has information via satellite connection, and the citizens living in the more developed areas have old fashioned telephones connected by wires. The people in the remote areas communicate by courier. There are no cell towers or internet providers that can be monitored by A I – and the New Siberians intend to keep it that way. We will be moving back in time to a society much like the one that you grew up in, Gram.

Drew, Diane, and I were among the first to apply for immigration on behalf of our families, and we have been awarded a land grant in a remote area just north of the Mongolian border.

We know how much the climate has changed here in North America, and the change has been even greater in Siberia. Land that was permafrost is now marshes, and farther south, where we will be, there are some places with microclimates that are even more temperate. One of these places is the area around Lake Baikal. "

What Marji remembers about National Geographic and the Wild Russia series is that Lake Baikal is the oldest and deepest lake in the world and that it holds the most fresh water. She understands.
"It's the water, isn't it Tommy?"

"We're going to need it, Gram; and within the next few generations it will be the most precious thing on Earth. Our valley is just to the south and east of the lake's outflow, on a tributary near the town of Ulan Ude. It's about as remote as you can get – and we will be starting our community from scratch, with only the tools that we bring with us."

Tommy laughs. "Of course, that's no small thing. We will have all of the supplies that we've been accumulating, as well as the equipment from the Alaska warehouse. But honestly, Gram, the supplies are the least of our resources. Our families are our greatest strength. We have two physicians, and medical professionals like my Mom and Dad, engineers and experts in agriculture, law and governance; scholars and teachers, and artists of every kind. And we have tradesmen – excellent tradesmen in architecture, masonry, mechanics, plumbing, carpentry, and solar technology. We even have a priest and a psychologist.

Our family group is actually the smallest – about fifty of us. Diane's family will be about 75, and God Bless him, Drew's family has 150 members. When you add in extended family and some close friends, we will have a diverse group of around 350 men, women and children."

Alaska - May 5, 2041

The past year has been a blur of activity. Marji hasn't been so busy since the days before the pandemic. By May 2040, Drew, Diane and Tommy had held the first of the family meetings. Marji's family met in Las Vegas for her annual birthday reunion, but instead of a party they used their Medic Alerts to finalize their plans. And then in June 2040, Tommy, Drew and Diane graduated from their Service Training and were given their new assignments in Alaska. They are managing communications and setting up the rendezvous site. Diane is their Chief of Operations.

At their family meetings, each group decided who they would invite to join them; and they selected their leaders. Tommy instructed everyone in the proper use of their "Medic Alert" jamming devices. "Be watchful and be very careful when you use these," he cautioned. "The A I system maintenance has been neglected, and the network is not as reliable as it used to be, but there are still places where the population is closely monitored. If you are uncertain about being watched, just touch your medallion. We have allies and safe places – you will recognize them by the symbol on all of your charms. It is just a stylized design of the Cyrillic letters 'N' and 'S' for New Siberia. You can trust anyone who shows you this symbol.

Depending on their ages and their roles, the combined family groups will be transferring to Alaska in three waves. The first wave is comprised of working-age adults and their families. Some will have travel permits, but the majority of these families are quietly dropping off the grid and becoming nomads. Over the past year, as they blend into the nomadic culture, they will make their way over land to their designated rendezvous in Alaska.

The second wave is comprised of the farmers and ranchers. This smaller group will be called upon (by the Chief of Operations) to transport their equipment, seeds and root stock, livestock, and their families. Their transport will be by various tractor trailer rigs dispatched by The Service.

The third wave, and the last scheduled to meet up at the Alaska rendezvous, will be the family elders. They will be going via travel permits on various cruise ships in May 2041.

Marji is 92, she is the oldest of all the new immigrants, and she was not eager to come. She recalls the heated argument that she had with her family last year when she announced at their meeting that she would not be a burden to them and that she would stay in her neighborhood to deal with whatever anarchy brought upon her. Obviously, she'd lost that one. They would not leave her behind. Tommy had insisted that emmigrating in whole family groups was essential to establishing their new culture, and, contrary to the attitudes during the Pandemic, their elders are not expendable.

And so it is that on May 5, 2041, Marji is standing with her luggage and her friend Marie on the dock of the Princess Cruise Line terminal in Seward, Alaska. Soon she will be embarking on a "whale watching expedition" that will take her and the other newly arrived elders to their designated meeting site. A freighter has been engaged to take the immigrants, their equipment, and all of their provisions to Japan and then on to New Siberia. By midsummer, they will all arrive at Lake Baikal to establish their colony.

There are some feral cats plying their trade along the dock, and as they pass one of the pilons, a kitten meows at them. Is it just human nature that your strongest memories are of your regrets? Her thoughts instantly go back 40 years in time to when she was working as a pest control technician. One of her customers lived in a new house along a green belt. Marji did not like this woman – her home was dirty and cluttered, and she was kind of flaky. On one monthly service call, the woman told her that a feral cat had kittens in her garage. And sure enough, a kitten was sitting on the coffee table in the living room. When Marji walked by, the kitten started meowing at her. "Does she always do this?" Marji laughed. "Oh no," the woman replied. "I've never heard her do this. Her name is Helen. If you want her, you can take her with you."

At the time Marji had two dogs, two jobs, a house, and a travel schedule to maintain. Her practical sense told her that she couldn't adopt a kitten. Still, she felt bad, and the next month when she made the service call, she asked her customer about Helen. The woman casually replied, "Oh, she's gone. Probably a coyote."

Marji stops and speaks softly to the meowing kitten on the dock in front of her. "I will name you Helen." Then she picks up the kitten, puts her into the pet carrier, and transfers Penny to her pocket.

Then Marji drapes her arm around her best friend's shoulder and looks out across the bright water to New Siberia. The rebellious act of picking up a stray kitten has broken the spell. Her dystopian existence of the past twenty years is over. She is free again. She will be surrounded by her family. She will spend her summer and autumn days helping the colony in all the ways that she can. And when it is finally her wintertime, she will pass away in her chair by the fire with a cat named Helen purring in her lap.

Soul Nourishing Visit

By Barbara Miller

It is December 21st, 2020, and I am driving
to the airport, my son Jeff sitting next to me.
We are conversing, and the drive seemed
awfully short. Felt torn in half, I wanted to
have geographic local access to him, and I
wanted him to safely go home to his amazing
family. He came to Las Vegas ignoring my
pleas to him that it was a bad time to come
because of the nationwide Corona pandemic.
So, I showed no sadness while we were quickly
getting closer to the airport. I hugged him very
hard, and off he went. And for the first time in
my nearly in the thirty years of living in Las
Vegas, I did not sob knowing I was going to
miss him; he is an amazing man.

The Lyft car stopped in front of my house,
and I saw my son for the first time since
February 2020. That first hug was euphoric,
surreal and wonderful. When I started
breathing again, we went into the house. The
deal we both agreed to was that we were going
nowhere. That was so we could stay safe from

the nightmare we were living. My friends all wanted to see him; however, they realized that would not be a good idea. That led to six days of just the two of us. He unpacked and showered immediately to wash off anything on his trip that might possibly be dangerous. Lunch was served and then he started on the honey-do list. I needed a new Mac computer and iWatch and iPad. Jeff went to my computer to see if we could find out where in town, we could get them. I had been trying to get an Apple appointment, and there was none for a month. I needed all of them while he was here so that he could set everything up for me. It is a perk for paying for college. It is December 15th, 2020, and I am standing on my driveway awaiting the Lyft car that is driving my son, Jeff, to me. He had called me in September to let me know that he had bought airline tickets to come to Las Vegas to spend time with me. As the pandemic was spreading like wildfire across the country, I was apprehensive, no frightened, for him to travel. He called me a few days before to tell me that he was definitely coming. At that point I agreed he should come. Jeff took a Covid test two weeks before he came and was negative both times. He tested while he was here and four days after he came home, all negative.

Jeff's brother, Howie died on December 19th, 2013, and that was the main reason he wanted to be here with me on that day, so that we could share it together. We bought some white balloons the morning of the 19th and released them to go up to Howie. We shared the grief and then we shared our memories of Howie as we watched the balloons ascend.

Jeff went on the Apple website and was searching for what we needed and saw that you could buy what we needed from the Summerlin Apple store, and it would be delivered. If I used my Apple credit card, I could get a three percent discount on my entire purchase, and they would give me a trade in of $190. I was so happy because we did not even have to go out to the store. One and a half hours later, the bell rang and had all the things I ordered. I was in shock; the human victrola was speechless. Jeff had the new computer and iPad and IWatch all set up and ready to go by dinner time. It is amazing what you can accomplish when you know what you are doing.

Which brings me to dinner and food in general. Jeff is six feet four and can carry weight and not look obese. I was taken aback when I saw him because he is so slim, he lost a ton of weight on his new eating regimen. He promised me that all his labs test were fine. Jeff told me on the phone before he came that he was on a no carb diet, so I filled the fridge appropriately. In the AM, it's bacon and cheese and eggs. Dinner is meat and Cole slaw and done. Preparing dinner was a breeze. Jeff grilled ribs, New York steak, salmon and tri-tip steak. I had prepared chicken cacciatore which is on his diet. Snacks were nonexistent. The dishes were done in minutes and on to relaxing and a movie. On Sunday, the day before he left, he decided he wanted to put in floodlights and a camera on either side of the outside garage doors. We went to Costco and guess who I saw standing in line to pay for her purchases? My dear friend Diane and her daughter Karen, in person. It was so good that at least we had that short time of in person conversation. We bought the lights, and in one hour I had flood lights and a camera that I can control from my phone. Life is good.

We talked about everything and anything. The best part of the conversations turned out to be me realizing how emotionally close we are. I stopped thinking of Jeff as my little boy and embraced an amazing adult. This trip turned out to be a realization that I do not need to ever feel that he is far away. He is always here in my home and heart.

Jeff called when he landed in New York, and my granddaughter Emily picked him up at the airport. Just like that, the visit was over however, we have memories of a heart healing six day visit that will last me a lifetime. I am very blessed.

Finding Time

By Diane Crane

Anne didn't go out much these days, and when she did, it was to visit the grocery store, not that she made that trip very often. It was just her. She was alone now.

The kids were grown and had moved away, chasing their own ambitions. She was glad that they were strong enough to be out on their own, living their lives, and Anne was independent enough to enjoy their visits but didn't need or want them to spend their energies on her well-being. It was enough that they loved each other.

While the pandemic had stolen their visits, they all kept in close touch, sharing their lives and supporting each other, if only by phone or email.

And that was enough.

That left Anne with time on her hands. Being home alone for months, she noticed things that needed to be done around the house. Neal had passed four years ago, and while Anne was pretty handy, Neal was the one who was the fixer. His tools still had their place neatly organized in the garage. They were there if she needed them.

So, over the last ten months, Anne had taken on various projects that never seemed to make their way to the top of her priority list. Sure, it took Anne more time to figure things out, but in the end, she conquered that leaky faucet and fixed that squeaky spot in the floor by the stairs. As time went on, she took to painting the kitchen and even bleached the grout in the floor, which had darkened over the years. She gave every baseboard in the house a fresh coat of paint and marveled at the difference it made. She stripped the powder room of that weary-looking wallpaper and then painted it a cheerful yellow. When that was done, she rescued some of the pictures that were propped upon the wall in the garage for years, having never really found a place inside the house.

She spent a whole week making her coveted strawberry jam. Those jars would come in handy when she needed a quick gift for a neighbor's birthday. She dusted off her sewing machine and finally made curtains out of that fabric she bought with good intentions but never got around to using. But there eventually came a time when Anne ran out of projects. There was really nothing more to be done around the house. And as she sat in the parlor, she felt quite self-satisfied. The pandemic had provided her with time to explore her capabilities and confirm her independence, if only to herself.

But there was one thing she hadn't focused on: Anne. That was an indulgence for which she never found time.

Last Christmas, her daughter had given her a set of those bath bombs, which, of course, Anne never used. There was never time. And her son had gifted her an expensive bottle of champagne for her last birthday, which she never found occasion to open. There were any number of presents scattered around the house for which Anne never found time. She giggled as she scurried around the house collecting the lot of them. There were fragrant candles and a jar of body butter and that silly romance novel that was collecting dust on the bookshelf. There was an unopened jar of face cream and some bottles of brightly colored nail polish that Anne had bought on a lark but had never quite gotten the courage to use.

Now she had the time, and there were no more excuses. As Anne turned on the bathtub faucet.She strategically placed and lit the candles, dropped that bath bomb in the tub and popped the cork on that champagne bottle. She poured herself a glass, and as she sipped, she smiled and wondered why it had taken her so long.

Another Perspective

Janet Feldman

The Covid experience has left me unsettled in my opinions about humankind. I have always chosen to see people as individuals, part of that coming naturally to me, and partially due to my training as a psychotherapist and the "unconditional positive regard" we were taught was the way to approach every new client.

With the pandemic, people seem to be falling into labeled categories which, although having validity, can also result in a viewpoint of "us against them," an already existing situation created in part by the extraordinary political divide, which itself was created, in my opinion, by an extraordinary amount of misinformation intended to manipulate people by causing fear and chaos, which it has. The fact that an extreme medical crisis has been politicized is despicable. A war of words has become a war of worlds, "ours versus theirs."

We have all heard of the "heroic" medical workers and their courageous responses to the pandemic, including risking their lives to save others, and too often falling victim to the disease themselves, making the ultimate sacrifice. A physician was recently speaking about this on a news program, reminding the listeners that these courageous people are no different from anyone else, that they have lives and families beyond the hospital wards, and that as courageous as they are, they are also afraid and exhausted, physically and emotionally.

The doctor made a request, so simple yet so impossible. She asked people to respect the hard work of all of those who ran into the fray, not away from it. She asked people to make minor sacrifices by scaling down their holiday plans, minimizing contact with others and adhering to the safety guidelines we have all known for months.

Some people will abide by these conditions, but there are millions who will not. The rules, they believe, do not apply to them; the pandemic is not as dangerous as it's made out to be; the numbers are made up. I am outraged that people have died and will continue to die due to the selfishness and ignorance of others.

It is astonishing to me that so many people are so self-absorbed that human suffering has no impact on them. At this moment, millions of people are facing eviction and homelessness; millions of people in this country and elsewhere are "food insecure," a term which has bothered me since I first heard it. To me it sounds like a diagnosis, rather than a situation. Why can't we just say, "people have nothing to eat." They are not "insecure;" they are desperate and starving.

My expression of outrage does nothing to ameliorate the situation. I'll continue to do what I can to keep myself safe, to donate and to volunteer remotely. I have little hope that when this virus is suppressed, the people who have been so cavalier about it will have altered their views. More likely they will say, "see, it wasn't so bad; I didn't get it." Nothing I can do or say will change that, and I, like millions of others, will mourn the loss of family, friends and those we once considered strangers.

Vaccination

Peter Philander

The virus makes our world ever smaller. At first, none of us knew a single person who had become sick from the viral infection, let alone anybody who had died of it. But as the number of positive cases has grown, having now, at the end of 2020, reached more than 20 million, one out of every sixteen Americans has tested positive for the virus, and more than 350,000 people have died. The rate at which new people are infected is increasing rapidly, and the number of people dying is also increasing rapidly.

Furthermore, the virus has evolved so that a new strain spreads more rapidly and is more contagious.

This is the time when all of us need to be especially careful of being infected or of spreading the infection. Unfortunately, this is also the time when we are tired of complying with the guidelines recommended by the infectious disease specialists.

We enter this phase with personal preferences and with some knowledge that we have acquired over the past year. Each of us has developed an attitude to the infection and we are beginning to have ingrained habits that dictate our behavior. Some of these come from what our caregivers told us during our childhood, some from what we studied as young adults and some from what we hear from sources that we trust and accept as authoritative.

The basic problem is that the way to limit every individual's exposure, is to make the social circle in which each person moves, ever smaller. Even within that circle, limit the ones with whom air is exchanged ever more strictly. This goes against most impulses of human behavior. First, we stopped shaking hands when meeting people. And we stopped hugging family and close friends. The very choice of separation and distancing is nearly anti-social. We are told to limit social contact to talking at a distance, while wearing a mask.

The behavior we would previously have frowned on and would have tried to teach our children not to engage in, is now embraced as the social norm. We isolate people in nursing homes and assisted living facilities and expect that they will tolerate being alone and with only electronic media for company. The behavior that the most nerdy and lonely gamers exhibit has become the norm for which we are all supposed to aim.

This pandemic resembles global warming in that each individual's personal choices contribute to an overwhelming tsunami of change. As with global warming, small changes in behavior will contribute to the greater goal of preserving our planet or decreasing the infection rate.

Sporting events have been among the first group activities that changed: large crowds were eliminated. Audiences were limited to people watching on television. Doctors' offices, notorious for having people wait to be seen, have adapted their schedules and the way patients are evaluated and treated. Schools and universities have resorted to internet-based teaching.

The choice still comes down to the individual and personal behavior. How does one explain that a city like Sidney, Australia, with a climate very similar to Los Angeles or Miami, has managed to have a low infection rate with only occasional spikes in the number of cases? Perhaps the explanation is simply that Australia has a population of around 25 million and is effectively an island that was isolated and closed off to visitors.

On the issue of personal choices, wearing a mask is the obvious, most important factor. This has been debated and discussed ad infinitum, and it has become a political statement, but the conclusion is inescapable.

Shopping is a popular pastime. The major season for gift-giving has passed, so the large department stores are now less tempting. Grocery stores are, however, a constant draw. It is obvious that one should limit the number of visits and should go when few other people are there. Is it essential that shopping should be done by people with fewer risk factors who are hired to do the activity? This is debatable but possibly optimal.

Eating out should be avoided. Ordering take-out food is an option. Hand washing and general good hygiene is important.

Vaccines are now available. The odds are simple. Covid-19 will cause severe illness and even death in somewhere around one in a hundred people who get infected. The vaccine may cause side effects in one in a million people or fewer of those vaccinated. Get vaccinated as soon as it is available.

Author Biographies

Janet Feldman, a New Jersey native and semi-retired psychotherapist, has been writing sporadically since grade school. A journalism degree led her to work as an editor, and as a freelance writer for medical magazines. She currently focuses on short fiction that highlights the behavior and interaction of people and considers herself grateful and fortunate to enjoy the camaraderie of this writing group.

Marjorie (Marji) Bleam has been a member of OLLI since her retirement six years ago. She joined the Creative Writing Class "in order to write better Christmas letters" but the friendships and encouragement soon became a pandemic lifeline.

 **Diane Crane** is a native New Yorker, born and raised in Manhattan. Diane relocated to Las Vegas some seven years ago to escape the cold and the snow but never imagined becoming part of a talented group of writers and genuinely exceptional people whose friendship is nothing short of remarkable. In addition to writing, she spends the majority of her retirement creating art.

 **Peter Philander** is a retired family physician who has lived in Las Vegas with his wife, Natalie, since 1998. He has been writing for most of his life and his audience consists of his peers,grandchildren and children.

Barbara Cooperstein-Miller was born and raised in Brooklyn, New York. She spent fifty years going through school, getting married and raising two amazing sons. She moved to Las Vegas at the age of fifty and started a new career in the medical field, retired at age seventy-seven and started writing. She discovered that writing gave her great pleasure and led her to some wonderful people.

Elizabeth Mackey lives with her husband and young children in Madison, Wisconsin, where she works as an attorney. Most of her writing consists of legal briefs and motions, but she enjoys writing short fiction, and one day hopes to write longer fiction, too.

 **Michael Pavesi** is a 69-year-old escapee from the Bronx, explaining his identifiable accent. He lives with his best friend Diane and their 3 outrageously cute cats. It is amazing, he thinks, how many people can disregard common sense practices intended to control the spread of disease and claim it's their constitutional right to such stupidity.

 **Drue Kramer** spent her child raising and working life in Michigan. She and her husband, Phil, moved to northern California ten years ago, to be closer to their grandchildren. She writes for her peers, children and grandchildren. Her other passion is creating pottery.

Ritha Burroughs taught special children for forty years. Now that she is retired, she has more time to write short stories about her travels around the world. The Write People have challenged her by thinking and writing outside of the box. Her participation with this group during the pandemic has been just Write.

Acknowledgements

With great appreciation to Grayson Ekman for his invaluable assistance in putting this project together. The rest of us technologically challenged "write people" could not have done this without his assistance.